Birth Mix Patterns

Birth Mix Patterns

Astrology, Numerology, and
Birth Order and their Effects on the Past,
Present, and Future

M. A. Payton
Award-winning Author of
Adventures of a Mainstream Metaphysical Mom
and
"Soul"utions

The Left Side
Powell, Ohio

Interior body text is set in 12 point Centar by Pete Masterson, Æonix
Publishing Group, www.aeonix.com
Cover illustration by Prescott Hill

ISBN 0-9719804-2-x
LCCN: 2005924982

Published by
The Left Side
Asheville, North Carolina
www.theleftside.com

Printed in the United States of America

Contents

I.
The "ALLNESS" of the Masculine and Feminine Balance

Introduction

I have come to realize through life experiences and now confirmed to my satisfaction through research that we, as human beings, can only express ourselves to our fullest potential if we have supportive, loving people in our lives who understand the value of balancing the masculine and feminine, ying yang, or opposites. Some would say this isn't much of a discovery but think about it just a bit more deeply. This isn't only about being married to, living with, dating, enjoying the company of, volunteering or working with others. We can do this without even liking each other (even in marriage, unfortunately). It's about effectively balancing the masculine and the feminine as we make life choices that will inevitably affect history at all levels. Sure, we can do many things on our own pretty well (and can do a lot of swimming upstream in the process) but not ALL things. So one way to experience the "ALLNESS" is to create a win:win which requires more compromise and empathy, resulting in less struggle, and increased balance. Put in even simpler terms… Let's all get along!

To help each other achieve this goal, I've identified a universal mix that has the potential to help us all have a clearer understanding of why we and others do what we do. *Birth Mix Patterns* takes familiar processes and creates a snapshot that we can comprehend on our own quickly! Using thousands of year-old tools called Astrology and Numerology together with Birth Order, I reveal various patterns. I (and thousands of others) have found this information to be helpful personality indicators. I've been "spot on" (as quoted from a radio caller from Australia) during radio shows, individual sessions and workshops helping clients set goals, understand (family, personal and business) small groups in various settings, and more.

Let's clarify that this is a starting point. It's not the end all and a way to make excuses. It is a beginning of many other beginnings that you will experience in this lifetime. It supports the idea that human beings are not complex, we simply create complex situations. We have basic motivations that connect us to all areas of life that can be revealed through Astrology Sun Signs, Numerology Life Paths, Birth Orders, and in-the-moment influences like Earth season changes and Personal Years. This handbook demonstrates *Birth Mix Patterns* through research of historical people— Presidents and First Ladies of the United States, royalty, civil rights leaders, entertainers and their companions and more. We gain clarity on how these Birth Mixes influenced the past and this gives us a glimpse into the future as history tends to repeat itself. Inevitably, this helps us to wake up, live more consciously, to celebrate, enhance, develop and/or alleviate traits empowering us to serve ourselves and others with balance.

Opening the Patriarchy Doors
to Experience "ALLNESS"

In a male-dominated world, there's a lot of data available on the history of (literally) "man." Researching feminine contributions, there is a tendency to overlook or under report achievements and other historical information. Once found, it was clear that those who valued and acknowledged the feminine and masculine voices equally were more successful in all aspects of life.

With this process, be comfortable in having to label personality traits to understand how to use this information most effectively. This profiling concept is similar to traveling—we have to know the beginning point to know how to get to the next destination. These are introductory trends that can help mark our progress and understand ourselves and others more clearly to create soul balance in ourselves, and ultimately to experience "ALLNESS."

Try this on for size. Experience how it fits. Then you make the determination.

"OH... I'M CHRISTIAN."

I was talking to someone who studied Birth Order intensely and I mentioned Astrology and Numerology as an additional reference point. One response was, "Oh, I'm a Christian."

Let's acknowledge that this book is not taking a religious position. It is simply another way to get a handle on who we are and how we interact to better the quality of our and others' lives. If something doesn't fit for you, you'll know it. This is a Universe of free will.

I became interested in Birth Order when reading material in relation to Adult Children of Alcoholics (growing up with an alcohol and drug abusing father). I was amazed at how accurately I and my siblings played out our roles within the abusive household drama. I hated to admit this but we were actually "text book." As I went on to study functional Birth Order (Birth Order trends less dependent of dysfunctional family patterns), it became even more telling universally. Patterns emerged in many regards—who tends to be more fun loving, who is most likely to be President of the United States, who is most accurate, who is likely to be a rebel....

Then I found acceleration points in connection to Birth Order when digging deeper into New Age (or better put, Old Age) ideas. For instance, a youngest child might be an uncontrollable partier if it is blended with certain Astrology and Numerology personality patterns. In regards to Astrology and Numerology, no one really knows why either of these thousands of year old arts is accurate, but they seem to pinpoint certain personality traits as well as how this relates to the past, present and future. Each of these studies can get very intricate and those who have mastered these arts have taken decades to get there.

Put It All Together and What Do You Get?

This all comes together in a neat little package. While I've created layers of information, I have found a way to decrease the complexity of Astrology, Numerology, Birth Order and Earth Cycles so that we can get a quick and clear understanding of why we (and others) do what we do on a daily basis. This doesn't replace the value of having a more detailed analysis in any one of these fields or seeking professional counseling. It's a way to help manifest your optimal reality financially, intellectually, physically, socially, and spiritually where you feel it fits (a concept called F.I.P.S.S. that I introduced in my book *"Soul"utions*). You will find summary sheets on every

I. The "ALLNESS" of the Masculine and Feminine Balance

Birth Order, Sun Sign (Astrology), Life Path and Personal Year number (Numerology) as well as Earth Cycle influences. The only requirement is to have an understanding of basic arithmetic to use this reference book to identify your own as well as others' personality patterns to move through life more clearly, consciously, and with more empathy. The goal is to love who you are unconditionally and accept others for who they are as well.

II.
The Terms

This section will be revisited when you are interested in calculating your and others' information in Numerology, Astrology, Birth Order, and Earth Cycle influences. A theme, the roles you take on as a result of those themes, how each mix influences us for the best and the challenges are also covered to build a profile. In addition, you'll have a general sense for how this impacts financial, intellectual, physical, social and spiritual well being.

NUMEROLOGY LIFE PATH NUMBER

This is connected to the day, month and year of birth and is the single most important calculation in your Numerology chart. It summarizes your life—the challenges, karma, lessons and general personality trends. More intricate Numerology will utilize the letters of your birth name as well as current name. For our goal setting purposes, we will focus on the Life Path as a general guidance point. You calculate Life Path as follows:

August 15, 1963; Get each to lowest denominator (1-9, 11, 22 or 33)

1963 (year of birth); 1+9+6+3=19; 1+9=10; 1+0=1

8 (August month of birth); 8

15 (day of birth); 1+5=6

Final number: 1+8+6=15; 1+5=6 Life Path.

If any of the three numbers being calculated are 11, 22, or 33, then this would be the lowest denominator. The final number will be 1-9, 11, 22 or 33 (33 is very rare). For instance:

November 29, 1808;

1808 (year of birth); 1+8+0+8=17; 1+7=8

12 (month of birth); 1+2=3

29 (day of birth); 2+9=11... lowest denominator for this specific Life Path calculation

Final number: 8+3+11=22... lowest denominator for this specific Life Path calculation (1-9, 11, 22 or 33). This could also be considered 22/4.

NUMEROLOGY PERSONAL YEAR NUMBER

This is connected to the day and month of birth plus current year and gives you a feel for the trends you may experience during that calendar year. There are nine (9) Personal Year numbers to complete a growth cycle so if you live to be ninety-nine (99), you will live through eleven (11) Personal Year cycles. You calculate it as follows:

August 15, 2004 ;

2004 (current year); 2 + 0 + 0 + 4 = 6

8 (month); 8

15 (day); 1 + 5 = 6

Final number: 6 + 8 + 6 = 20; 2 + 0 = 2 Personal Year.

The lowest denominator for Personal Year calculation is 1-9.

ASTROLOGY SUN SIGN

This is connected to the day and month of birth only (time, place and year are not factors for this exercise). The sun is the core of the solar system and sustains all other planets. While more intricate Astrology provides much more detail (analyzing many other planets and "houses"), for our purposes, we will focus on our core of being, the ruling planet in our Astrology chart, the planet where we are most likely to come to terms with our true selves and happiness.

BIRTH ORDER

This is connected to the order of birth and role you played out within the family unit that raised you from infancy and beyond. There are differing opinions on Birth Order theories. It becomes quite intricate (as does Astrology and Numerology) as it takes into account years between births, gender Birth Order, physical/mental strengths and weaknesses (handicaps, body build, physical attractiveness...), size of family, adoption...

Some rules of thumb that a variety of experts embrace that have helped me in my baseline work:

If the siblings above you are both five years or more older and younger than you (and/or no siblings are below you or above you), you can take on Only child traits.

If you are second in birth line but the sibling above you is of opposite gender, you are also First Born but of the opposite gender and can take on First Born patterns.

If you are second in birth line but the sibling above you is handicapped, has problems with physical attractiveness/body build, you may take on the traits of First Born (switching Birth Order in essence).

If you are from a large family, the family units can run in fours (fourth born Youngest, eighth born family unit B Youngest...).

Middle children are not always predictable. They can be the pleasers or the rebels but are generally negotiators.

Adopted children can become rebellious at any order.

There are always exceptions to these rules and many, many, many opinions.

EARTH CYCLES

The four Earth Cycles (also known as four seasons) that influence our daily lives within a twelve month period are Spring Equinox, Summer Solstice, Fall Equinox and Winter Solstice. The seasons change around the twentieth of March, June, September and December. Additional detail on Earth Cycles can also be found in my books Adventures of a Mainstream Metaphysical Mom and "Soul"utions.

ACCELERATION POINTS

This occurs when one or more of the Birth Mix elements (Astrology, Numerology and Birth Order, as well as in-the-moment influences) accelerate a particular personality theme or pattern. These points can become life strengths or challenges. For instance, a Leo can be very generous, Life Path six takes care of people, and first born is the boss and, sometimes, organizer, caregiver or parent of younger siblings. In this instance, the challenge is to not become an enabler by over caring (Leo, "Six"), and having money problems due to generosity (Leo, "Six"). This combination can also result in being adored for being so giving (Leo, "Six"), and known for being reliable (First Born, "Six").

PERSONALITY/YEAR OR EARTH CYCLE THEME

What inspires you at the core… pushes you in a particular direction.

ROLE

An acting out of your theme.

BEST AT

Your strengths.

CHALLENGE(S)

Personality diamonds in the rough to become conscious of. Over time, these can be indicators of new strengths/personal developments.

F.I.P.S.S. BALANCE

A process that looks at all areas of life— Financial, Intellectual, Physical, Social, and Spiritual—to create soul balance. Financial connects with anything having to do with money. Intellectual connects with any conscious information coming into our lives in relation to study/education, travel, training, and /or expanding our minds. Physical connects with anything to do with nurturing the physical body. Social connects with all relationships in the physical (most intimate inner circle to distant outer circle). Spiritual connects to the inner self/child, self-happiness, self-worth, non-physical. Additional details on the F.I.P.S.S. goal setting process can be found in my book *"Soul"utions.*

III.
It's All in the Mix

Numerology Life Path Influences

Numerology in its simplest terms is using numbers to understand your personality patterns and life themes. This can be done, primarily, by using the numbers associated with your birth date, and assigning numbers to the letters in your name. There are endless pieces of information that can be extrapolated from the numbers but we will only focus on the number that serves as a personality summary.

We'll look at Life Path numbers "1" through "9, 11, 22," and "33." We'll have a better understanding of how the numbers influence history by:

- Identifying people who have gone down in history who are associated with each number
- Sharing a short story about an accomplished person to further demonstrate the personality pattern
- Summarizing the patterns of each Life Path number so that you might be able to use these to identify our own and others' patterns

#1 — The Leader... "Follow me!"

"The inevitable end of multiple chiefs is that they fade and disappear for lack of unity."

—*Napoleon I, Maxims (1804-15)*

With few exceptions, the Life Path One dislikes being told what to do. If they perceive being forced into something, the hair on the backs of their "leader" necks stand on end. They want to be the boss rather than be bossed. These are your "can do" people who prefer room to break ground that they can call their own.

Additional ways to describe "the leader" include one with a great deal of inner strength, independent, pioneer, creator, with a life challenge of being a bit self-absorbed and intense. Because leaders have a natural ability to satisfy material needs and achieve a position of status, they are drawn to professions, people, and situations that allow them to manage.

Three Presidents of the United States were ones and were only found in the nineteenth century—William McKinley, Zachary Taylor, and George Washington (our first United States President). Two of the "Ones" met their demise while in the Oval Office—McKinley (described as a person representing the newer view), and Zachary Taylor (called "Old Rough and Ready"). Washington lived out his terms and was named the "Father of his Country" (great for a number one). We've had one First Lady (in the twentieth century—Claudia Johnson) to join the ranks of number "one." She was known to have been bossed around by her husband in public and, consequently, not really able to find her balance point while in the White House.

A famous "One" who balanced the feminine energy was Florence

Nightingale. With the additional qualities of a Taurus Sun Sign (the stable force) and the Youngest Born (the charmer) in her family, she would have a potential personality mix of a "can do," charmer with the ability to manage chaos in the midst of any storm. She and her sister were well-educated and privileged but she felt that she was led by God to aggressively pursue her place in history (rather than simply being a smart match for a suitor).

Florence Nightingale is most known for being a pioneer in nursing and reformed hospital sanitation methods in a time when Victorian women didn't pursue a professional career (did they try to tell a "One" not to do something again?). Through her formal education and natural talents, she also created a statistical analysis technique that visually graphed the number of preventable deaths in the military (number management is a "One" specialty). She reformed the British military health-care system by visually demonstrating, through her "polar-area diagram," the number of needless deaths caused by unsanitary conditions. She developed a record-keeping system that improved city and military hospitals and saved many lives. Nightingale's ground-breaking statistical processes earned her the title of Fellow of the Royal Statistical Society in 1858 and was an honorary member of the American Statistical Association in 1874.

To summarize top-line traits of the Life Path "One:"

LIFE PATH 1 — THE LEADER

Personality Theme: Being ahead. Do it better and faster. Seek finer things.

Role: Provider. Leader.

Best at: Being own boss.

Challenge(s): Taking orders from others. Following. Finding value in listening.

F.I.P.S.S. (FINANCIAL, INTELLECTUAL, PHYSICAL, SOCIAL, SPIRITUAL):

F—Strong when can demonstrate management skills, when has control. Hard work is expression of status.

I—Strong when can express pioneer spirit and fulfill goals.

P—Strong when maintain food/exercise program as this physical accomplishment demonstrates ability to lead. Many enjoy competitive activities to stay in shape.

So—Strong when connects with others, and their opinions, and is less self-absorbed.

Sp—Strong when learns to appreciate life overall and less for appearance.

Famous 1's: Emperor Napoleon Bonaparte (French military leader), Sir Sean Connery (actor, "James Bond"), Billy Joel (musician, songwriter), Jerry Lewis (actor, philanthropist), Leonardo Da Vinci (painter, inventor, genius visionary), Walt Disney (artist, creator of Disney cartoons and related properties), Elizabeth Dole (senator, 2000 U.S. Presidential hopeful/never ran), Martin Luther King (civil rights leader), Sir Isaac Newton (mathematician, scientist), Maria Montessori (educator and creator of Montessori education process), Florence Nightingale (nurse and reformed British health care system), U.S. First Lady Claudia Johnson, U.S. Presidents— William McKinley, Zachary Taylor, and George Washington (first United States President).

#2 — The Inward Creator/Motivator...
"It's what's inside that counts."

"A (wo)man who listens because (s)he has nothing to say can hardly be a source of inspiration. The only listening that counts is that of the talker who alternately absorbs and expresses ideas."

—**Agnes Repplier, *The Luxury Of Conversation,***
Compromises (1904)

One United States President in the twentieth century was a pure Life Path "Two"—Calvin Coolidge (the other President, William Henry Harrison, was only in office for one month so I didn't count him). However, four other Presidents were "Eleven/Twos" (see Life Path "11/2" for details). Coolidge was known to be a man of few words (not unusual to see in "Twos"). His claim, during his inaugural address, was that the United States had achieved "a state of contentment never before seen" and his twoness goal was to keep it that way. These are the naturals for keeping the peace. But don't mistake them as being weak. Their styles to accomplish their goals are just a bit more subdued. The "Two" First Ladies were quietly aggressive in office. Unfortunately, Florence Harding (caught up in scandal) and Julia Tyler (only in office eight months to enjoy her lavish parties) didn't have the opportunity to make as much of a positive impact. These are the inwardly creative and have the potential to manifest to perfection in many ways.

When you add a little fire in the Sun Sign or First Born energy in the mix, you get someone like Amelia Earhart. She was a "Two," Leo Sun Sign. She was the first woman to fly across the Atlantic Ocean solo (Leo leader) but also had a two perseverance as a volunteer nurse in World War 1 as well as being a social worker. While being a nurse and social worker seem more of a feminine expression in a patriarchy accepted role, this becomes more significant when we know that Ms. Earhart was independently wealthy — through inheritance as a young woman as well as married into money. As a two she fulfilled her need to heal; create balance and peace in the world. Her drive to be a leader as a pilot would have fulfilled her Leo, First Born path.

Here are some of the personality patterns you may observe with a "Two:"

LIFE PATH 2 — THE INWARD CREATOR/MOTIVATOR

Personality Theme: The perfect tranquil environment.

Role: Counselor. The bringer of balance within diverse situations.

Best at: Team motivating. Listening. Inward creativity.

Challenge(s): Overt leading. Fully expanding own talents (tend to hold back to serve others and keep the peace).

F.I.P.S.S. (FINANCIAL, INTELLECTUAL, PHYSICAL, SOCIAL, SPIRITUAL):

F—Strong when can express perfectionist nature (possibly as a counselor, physical or massage therapist, hands-on healer, expressive creator, artist, author, communicator).

I—Strong when abilities are not underestimated by others.

P—Strong when overcomes pattern of gaining weight due to lack of self-involvement or excessive inward thinking. Balance lifestyle, combining realistic exercise while inwardly processing.

So—Strong when not as shy and can utilize diplomatic, tactful, sensitive, team player talents.

Sp—Strong when achieves harmonious internal and external environment. Great eye for beauty.

Famous 2's: Amelia Earhart (first woman pilot to cross the Atlantic solo), John Glenn (first astronaut on the moon, congressman), Dr. Sally Ride (first American woman in space to orbit earth), U.S. First Ladies—Florence Harding, Julia Taylor, U.S. President Calvin Coolidge.

#3 — THE INFORMED SPEAKER/COMMUNICATOR... "EVERYBODY LISTEN UP!"

"True conversation is an interpretation of worlds, a genuine intercourse of souls, which doesn't have to be self-consciously profound but does have to touch matters of concern to the soul."
—*Thomas Moore, Soul Mates (1994)*

Not to be confused with his father, the second United States President (John Adams), sixth President John Quincy Adams was nicknamed "Old Man Eloquent." It was very appropriate for the "Three" communicator. His role of being seen and, more importantly, heard is forever etched in history. In the ultimate "Three" style, John Q. died on the Congress floor in front of an audience. There were more U.S. First Ladies than President's with this Life Path, but only three served of the five. The two better known were Edith Roosevelt and Hillary Clinton in the twentieth century. Our U.S. President communicators included (both in the nineteenth century)—John Quincy Adams, Andrew Jackson and U.S. First Ladies—Hillary Clinton (became U.S. senator following her term as First Lady), Ellen Arthur (never served), Jane Pierce (disliked the White House), Edith Roosevelt (Teddy Roosevelt's wife), Hannah Van Buren (never served).

Anne Mansfield-Sullivan—a Life Path "Three," First Born girl, Aries—was dealt many life challenges unfamiliar to the former U.S. Presidents and First Ladies which included a combination of poverty, abuse,

Presidents that left the White House only to return four years later and this was largely due to his wife's drive to return. There were five First Ladies that shared Cleveland's Life Path. One of the more known and loved in our time included Betty Ford. She had many life challenges and became well-respected as a result of her ability to dig out of the trenches of alcohol and drug abuse and breast cancer.

"Fours" are great at putting things in order and aren't afraid (in fact, many times they prefer) to roll up their sleeves, and tackle a problem. They can wrap their minds around problems, and overcome limitations. For instance, try being a woman in the 1950's who is an expert on sex. These were the days when women were encouraged to fix their make-up and hair before their husbands made it home from a hard day at work! Being a pioneer in uncharted territory comes with hard knocks. Mary S. Calderone was an M.D. internationally recognized in the field of human sexuality. A Life Path "Four" and Cancer (comforter), she was president of the Sex Information and Education Council of the United States and co-founded this in 1954. For nearly thirty years she was executive director and president. Add to the controversy in this conservative time of being the medical director for the Planned Parenthood Federation of America (beginning in the early '50's) and you have a bundle of challenges (just what "Fours" thrive on).

She authored subjects like: *Questions and Answers About Sex and Love, Sexuality and Human Values, Manual of Family Planning and Contraceptive Practices, The Family Book About Sexuality,* and *Talking With Your Child About Sex.* A pioneer. A hard worker. One that established foundation, persevered in the face of adversity but was still able to create, process and accomplish realistic goals.

The "Four" that seems to have pushed herself into "Twenty-two" energy (see Life Path "22" for more information) is Oprah Winfrey. She is one of the most public figures in the United States in the twenty-first century as chairwoman of Harpo, Inc., Harpo Productions, Inc., Harpo Studios, Inc., Harpo Films, Inc., Harpo Print, LLC and Harpo Video, Inc. She has a long list of accomplishments for her acting (Academy Award and Golden Globe nominated), broadcasting (syndicated talk show, created successful television station "Oxygen"), publication (magazine founder and editorial director) and philanthropy work (foundations, scholarship funds and even has an "Oprah Law" for protection of abused children).

Any "Four" would relate to the statement that your strengths are also your life challenges. Creating order can decrease chaos. Creating order can also create controversy. Being fair (through "Four" eyes) can create equality, but will not be the only perspective.

Personality patterns of a "Four" can be as follows:

LIFE PATH 4 — THE REALIST, PROBLEM SOLVER, BUILDER OF ORDER

Personality Theme: Create order. Create method and process to overcome life challenges.

Role: Problem solver. Hard worker. Establish foundation.

Best at: Making decisions, organizing, persevering, being detailed and dependable.

Challenge(s): Scattering energy too far to solve too many problems at one time. Being too rigid or dogmatic.

F.I.P.S.S. (FINANCIAL, INTELLECTUAL, PHYSICAL, SOCIAL, SPIRITUAL):

F—Strong when energy is focused (not scattered and chaotic) and can express precision, discipline, method, order. Not afraid to work and put in long hours to build career, nest egg and can handle money carefully but can miss opportunities if too cautious and detailed (missing the big picture).

I—Strong when working with conventional ideas. Stronger when flexible in thinking and open to new ideas.

P—Strong when not overworking and apply same focus to health.

So—Strong when able to demonstrate their reliability, dependability, and loyalty. Great parent, life partner, friend.

Sp—Strong when process is clear. Personal growth hinges on ability to judge less harshly (being flexible with opposing ideas).

Famous 4's: Woody Allen (actor, director, writer), Emily Greene Balch (1946 Nobel Peace Prize winner/economist/social scientist), Bill Gates (MicroSoft founder), Mary Calderone (Planned Parenthood director, sex expert), Dr. Marie Curie (Nobel Peace Prize in advancement of chemistry), Sir Elton John (musician), Babe Ruth (pro baseball player), Arnold Schwarzenegger (weightlifter, actor, politician), Donald Trump (entrepreneur, real estate developer), U.S. First Ladies—Betty Ford, Lucy Hayes, Martha Jefferson (never served), Elizabeth Monroe, U.S. President Grover Cleveland, Oprah Winfrey (actress, magazine editor, entertainer/talk show host).

#5 — The Unending Talent... "What's new?"

"Talent is a question of quantity. Talent does not write one page: it writes three hundred."

—*Jules Renard, Journal, 1887, TR. Elizabeth Roget*

Four very dynamic Presidents were "Fives" — Thomas Jefferson, Abraham Lincoln, Teddy Roosevelt and Franklin D. Roosevelt. Thomas Jefferson was the creator of the words "All men are created equal. All men are entitled to life, liberty and the pursuit of happiness" within the Declaration of Independence. He was also the founder of the University of Virginia. Honest Abe was known for his time served during the Civil War — preserving the Union, enforcing the laws of the United States and issuing the Emancipation Proclamation that freed all slaves within the Confederacy. Teddy Roosevelt was America's first environmentalist President protecting over 190 million acres of forests, natural resources and wildlife, as well as being a "bully" activist on a wide range of subjects including morals, literature, art, marriage, divorce, birth control, and equal education for women. FDR, during his twelve year stint in office during the Great Depression and World War II, introduced the "New Deal" bringing the U.S. into national economic recovery as well as putting the U.S. into super power status when winning the war. The two President Roosevelts accounted for twenty years in the White House in the twentieth and twenty-first centuries (over one-hundred and seven years equating to nineteen percent). Just two U.S. First Ladies were similar Life Paths. One being an out-of-the-box thinker and avid learner (First Lady Fillmore) and the other was First Lady Nixon who distanced herself from the office to protect herself and husband.

Helen Keller was a very accomplished "Five" woman, inspiring and meeting many nations' leaders and disabled people in her lifetime. A Cancer Sun Sign (comforter) taking on more of a Youngest (charmer) role due to her life challenges is a great example of one conquering her disabilities, she achieved amazing things in her "Five" glory. By age one she was completely blind and deaf due to a childhood illness. Her parents, not knowing what to do with a disabled child, allowed her to become wild and untamable. After five years of this they finally brought in a teacher (Anne Sullivan) that could reach her. Within three years she could read and write Braille then she moved onto sign language. By the time she was sixteen she could communicate well enough to go to preparatory school and college (graduating with honors).

After college, Keller became concerned with the conditions of the blind and the deaf-blind and became active with the American Foundation for the Blind and the American Foundation for Overseas Blind. She appeared before legislatures, gave lectures, wrote many books (translated into more than fifty languages) and articles and created the Helen Keller Endowment Fund. She lectured in over twenty-five nations throughout the world including working with soldiers in World War II who had been blinded in the war.

Are "Fives" power houses? They can be. My observation of this Life Path is that their need for freedom can cripple their overall efforts unless they focus. When they do, you'll witness productive, dynamic, driven manifesters. However, they will manifest on their terms.

Here are some patterns you may witness with "Fives":

LIFE PATH 5 — THE UNENDING TALENT

Personality Theme: New experiences. Change. New Ideas. Freedom.

Role: Change Agent. Out-of-the-box on their terms.

Best at: Brainstorming. Innovation.

Challenge(s): Focus due to so many ideas and overall talent.

F.I.P.S.S. (FINANCIAL, INTELLECTUAL, PHYSICAL, SOCIAL, SPIRITUAL):

F—Strong when regularly experience new ideas, concepts, and people. Great in sales, advertising, PR, politics, self-employment (as long as stick to becoming an expert in a few areas rather than mastering none).

I—Strong when can experience/partake in all areas of life. Travel and adventure high on goal list.

P—Strong when disciplined on controlling food and other substance intake (too much adventure). Keep the body limber to match your limber/flexible (new, free, change) ideas energy.

So—Strong when feeling free to experience adventure, travel, variety.

Sp—Strong when not forced into conventional thought. Being less intense brings inner harmony.

Famous 5's: Charles Darwin (naturalist on evolution and natural selection), Vincent Van Gogh (painter), Hellen Keller (blind/deaf, author/speaker/mentor), Coretta Scott King (civil rights leader, Martin Luther King widow), Steven Spielberg (film director), U.S. First Ladies—Abigail Fillmore, Thelma "Pat" Nixon, U.S. Presidents—Thomas Jefferson, Abraham Lincoln, Theodore Roosevelt, Franklin D. Roosevelt.

#6 — The Responsible One/The Server...
"How can I help you?"

"To serve is beautiful, but only if it is done with joy and a whole heart and a free mind."

—Pearl S. Buck, Men And Women, To My Daughters With Love (1967)

We have a large population of "Six" U.S. Presidents in the twentieth and twenty-first century— George W. Bush, Dwight Eisenhower, Warren Harding, James Madison, Richard Nixon, Woodrow Wilson. In fact, by 2008, twenty-nine of the past one-hundred and seven years (since 1901) have been overseen by "sixes" (twenty-seven percent of the time). If you combine this with the feminine balance of Eleanor Roosevelt and Helen Taft (sixteen years in office), this would mean that forty-five years or forty-two percent of America's highest office has major "Six" influences. This would say that America has a strong bond to the "Cosmic Fathers/Mothers" and vice versa.

A woman who had much in common with fellow "Six" Woodrow Wilson and his support of the League of Nations (later becoming the United Nations) was Carrie Chapman Catt. She was a "Six" that played a leading role in women gaining the right to vote and in 1920 founded the League of Women Voters. Multi-faceted in the service industry, she was also the first woman in the nation to be appointed superintendent of schools, and the first female newspaper reporter in San Francisco. Catt helped organize the International Woman Suffrage Association alongside Susan B. Anthony and later founded the National Committee on the Cause and Cure of War.

Taking a more specific look at "Six" patterns:

LIFE PATH 6 — THE RESPONSIBLE ONE/THE SERVER

Personality Theme: Serving others. Compassionate.

Role: Cosmic Mother or Father. Organizer to help others accomplish goals/heal.

Best at: Leading charismatically and reliably.

Challenge(s): Interfering or saving others too much. Creatively expressing him/herself fully. Over tasking.

F.I.P.S.S. (FINANCIAL, INTELLECTUAL, PHYSICAL, SOCIAL, SPIRITUAL):

F—Strong when develop reliable tools to help others and can utilize personal charm and charisma to create success in business, organizations and events.

I—Strong when connected to personal growth as well as need to serve others.

P—Strong when control cravings for dairy and sweets. Generally graceful and attractive.

So—Strong when express counseling side functionally versus controlling. Accept love in return for service. Great life partner and parent.

Sp—Strong when overcome seeing self as "savior" (taking that weight off your shoulders) and thrive on spiritual returns as a result of kindness and generosity.

Famous 6's: Joan of Arc (martyr, saint), Sandra Day O'Connor (first woman U.S. Supreme Court Justice) Thomas Edison (inventor—light bulb and devices to expand usage, alkaline battery, motion picture camera...), Albert Einstein (genius inventor, $E=MC^2$), Michael Jackson (award-winning singer, songwriter), Reverend Jesse Jackson (civil rights leader, non-violent), Stephen King (author), John Lennon (musician, songwriter, peace advocate), U.S. First Ladies—Rachel Jackson (never served), Eliza

Johnson, Eleanor Roosevelt, Helen Taft, U.S. Presidents—George W. Bush, Dwight Eisenhower, Warren Harding, James Madison, Richard Nixon, Woodrow Wilson, Stevie Wonder (musician/blind/known as musical genius).

#7 — THE SOURCE OF KNOWLEDGE. EXPERT, THINKER, ANALYZER… "I HAVE THE ACCURATE ANSWER."

"Common sense suits itself to the ways of the world. Wisdom tries to conform to the ways of Heaven."
—Joseph Joubert, Pensees (1842), 8.6, TR. Katharine Lyttelton

"Seven" is a number of mastery. Some would say that double digit master numbers hold even more intensity ("11, 22," and "33") than other numbers, and can be difficult to integrate into a physical life (can get easier with age). So Life Path "Sevens" can have a difficult time adjusting to the physical world at times. Alone time is important but too much alone time can create isolation—can be accidental due to people misunderstanding them or sometimes by choice. Many times "sevens" will be a true expert in, at least, one subject. They are very bright, intellectual, and intuitive and can become cynical if they experience "an answer" not fitting their life perspectives. They can have spurts of very social energy but look for "alone" shelter once they've reached their limits. If they have a more social or nurturing Astrology Sign or Birth Order, it seems to pull them into the world a bit more. Many times, they are pulled into the world a bit more by the people who love them. A very social relative of mine was dating a "Seven." The "Seven" said he liked dating her because she could carry on a complete conversation without his assistance.

Life Path "Seven" and "Eleven" combined are dominated by U.S.

First Ladies (eight to be exact) in contrast to the U.S. Presidents. In the twentieth and twenty-first centuries, fourteen years of U.S. Presidents and four years of First Ladies were "Sevens," or seventeen percent of one-hundred and seven years. Maybe it was easier for "Seven" U.S. First Ladies to integrate into a patriarchy because there was less pressure to perform as a woman. They learned to co-exist in the physical world with more ease (most being in the nineteenth century). Or maybe many of their stories weren't told. We know Mrs. Lincoln had one tragedy after another in her lifetime (loss of children as well as her husband). Two of the four U.S. Presidents, Garfield and Kennedy, were shot and killed in office. And many more famous faces seemed to have equally difficult times resulting in untimely deaths—Bruce Lee (drug overdose), John F. Kennedy, Jr. (plane crash while he was the pilot), and Marilyn Monroe (controversial drug overdose). And then there are the physical challenges that Muhammed Ali faces with Parkinson's. While at the same time all of these figures are remembered and are role models to the world.

So what does this mean if you are a "Seven?" The whole "Seven" world is not outlined on these few pages so don't feel like you will meet a dismal demise. It's important, however, that you recognize your need to be a central resource (expert) for your chosen field/hobby/profession and find positive ways to spread/communicate/share/utilize your knowledge base that will satisfy you as well as the receiver of information. Celebrate your time alone, and embrace that need. You may not be easy to get along with because your style can intimidate others and/or have the possibility of being misunderstood as a result of your communication style. Awareness and effective integration into the physical world is the key.

An interesting phenomena happened in 1917. Jeanette Rankin was the first woman elected to U.S. congress. In "Seven" style, refusing to acknowledge the physical world, this was *three years before women were guaranteed the constitutional right to vote.* She lost her seat on U.S. Congress because she voted against the war of that time and then ran and was elected in the 1940's in the House of Representatives (Twenty years in between elections were spent supporting peace and freedom). She ran on a platform of peace and kept her word. She was the only member of congress that voted "no" for entering World War II. Rankin also voted "no" to enter into war with the Japanese once they bombed Pearl Harbor. This was so unpopular that she had to seek refuge in a phone booth until the police could come and escort her home. She spent her life advocating peace.

So taking a look at "Sevens:"

LIFE PATH 7 — THE SOURCE OF KNOWLEDGE. EXPERT/THINKER/ANALYZER

Personality Theme: Absorbing vast amounts of information to become an expert.

Role: Utilizing or sharing knowledge to create clarity for others, self, and/or events.

Best at: Exploring, thinking, and putting the pieces together for "truth."

Challenge(s): Being too guarded and self-centered. Not being open and trusting of others and their ideas.

F.I.P.S.S. (FINANCIAL, INTELLECTUAL, PHYSICAL, SOCIAL, SPIRITUAL):

F—Strong when expert information is useful to advancement.

I—Strong when have freedom to research independently, express creativity and come up with practical solutions independently.

P—Strong when control cravings for physical pleasures.

So—Strong when open to others' ideas and overcome being too isolated, alone, independent. Can be very charming when centered but look to come out of the limelight rather quickly.

Sp—Strong as age, and can be very connected with "spirituality."

Famous 7's: Muhammed Ali (prize fighter and Parkinson's mentor), Emily Dickinson (American lyrical poet), Lady Diana Spencer (Princess of Wales), John F. Kennedy Jr. (son of JFK), Bruce Lee (actor, martial arts expert), Marilyn Monroe (actress rumored to be having affair with JFK), Alice Paul (led Nineteenth Amendment of the constitution passage/authored Equal Rights Amendment), Jeanette Rankin (first woman to be elected to U.S. Congress), Peter Tchaikovsky (classical music composer), U.S. First Ladies—Louisa Adams, Caroline Harrison, Anna Harrison, Lou Hoover, Mary Lincoln, Ida McKinley, Sarah Polk, Edith Wilson, U.S. President's—George H. W. Bush, James Garfield, Benjamin Harrison, John F. Kennedy, Harry Truman.

#8 — The Material Manifester... "Waste Not, Want Not."

"A moderate addiction to money may not always be hurtful; but when taken in excess it is nearly always bad for the health."
—**Clarence Day**, *Improving the Lives of the Rich*,
The Crow's Nest (1921)

The "Eight" Life Path is sometimes confused with the idea that this path is destined to be a millionaire. What this is more likely to mean is if "Eights" need money for lunch and they have nothing in their pockets, they will take a couple of steps and find five dollars on the sidewalk (just enough to pay for lunch). But if they master their number, anything is possible.

There were a total of eight U.S. Presidents categorized as material manifesters. This Life Path was much more dominant in the nineteenth century, however. From 1817 to 1885, this equated to thirty-one of the sixty-eight years or thirty-one percent. The only "Eights" in office for the twentieth century inherited the office—Gerald Ford and Lyndon Johnson (Johnson was re-elected for another term). The six Presidents from the nineteenth century were Chester Arthur, Milliard Fillmore, Ulysses S. Grant, James Monroe, James Polk, Martin Van Buren. First Ladies included Laura Bush, Nancy Reagan (both serving eight years by 2008) and Julia Grant (the Grant first couple were both "Eights"), and Ellen Wilson.

Of course, being an "Eight," the ultimate symbol of wealth in the twentieth century would be the classic beauty Elizabeth Taylor. Elizabeth Taylor looked and played the part in movies and real life. By the time she was a teen-ager she was the top MGM child star and later multiple Oscar-winning adult actress and (reported) millionaire by the early 1960's. Mrs. Taylor also has an abundant number of marriages equaling, you guessed it, eight in this lifetime (counting one she married twice).

Some "Eight" patterns might include:

LIFE PATH 8 — THE MATERIAL MANIFESTER
Personality Theme: Accumulate wealth. Create wealth.
Role: Manager. Visionary.
Best at: Manifesting money or other means when needed.
Challenge(s): Holding onto wealth longer-term and effectively managing flow. Connecting to less material areas of life.

F.I.P.S.S. (FINANCIAL, INTELLECTUAL, PHYSICAL, SOCIAL, SPIRITUAL):
F—Strong when able to exercise long-range vision. Viewed as natural in business and management (politics, business, finance, law, science, manage large institutions) but can be greedy. Can have major highs and lows.

I—Strong when travel and/or exposed to beautiful things. Being formally and informally educated is key to image.

P—Strong when in optimal shape (is a personal sign of success/ strength).

So—Strong when can be in a role to inspire and guide others. Can be pushy and arrogant decreasing positive relationships.

Sp—Strong when can connect with humanity and inner happiness and less with power and money.

Famous 8's: Mary Cassatt (Impressionist painter), Princess Grace (Kelly) of Monaco, Michelangelo (artist), Pope John Paul II (Catholic Pope), Elizabeth Taylor (actress), U.S. First Ladies—Laura Bush, Nancy Reagan and Julia Grant (the Grant first couple were both "Eights"), Ellen Wilson, U.S. Presidents—Gerald Ford, Lyndon Johnson, Chester Arthur, Millard Fillmore, Ulysses S. Grant, James Monroe, James Polk, Martin Van Buren.

#9 — THE HUMANITARIAN... "THE MORE YOU GIVE, THE MORE YOU GET."

*"The place to improve the world is first in one's own heart and head
and hands, and then work outward from there."*
—*Robert M. Pirsig, Zen And The Art Of*
Motorcycle Maintenance (1974)

"Humanitarians" seem to prefer to have many friends. This personality sees the best in most people, so it has to be blatantly obvious that people are putting "Nines" in harm's way before they finally run the other way. Many humanitarians' friends may be heard saying, "He/she has had many hardships and they just don't deserve them... Why does this happen to him/her?" Humanitarians have to be sure that they are addressing the real world and not the picture they have in their heads on their "better world." Many "Nines" inherit money (which would include smart investment decisions as well as family money) and have sponsors/mentors that push them "up" in the world (a manager, a relative, a life partner...).

The most famous "Nine" U.S. First Couple of our time would be Jimmy and Rosalyn Carter. But "Nine's" have not been very prevalent in the U.S. Oval Office with four U.S. Presidents including James Buchanan, Rutherford Hayes, William H. Taft and two First Ladies including Margaret Taylor.

Being humanitarians, the Carter's would be the poster couple winning the Nobel Peace Prize. Deserving (according to a number of supporters) of the Nobel Peace Prize but never awarded was Gandhi, who sacrificed his life to achieve peace. Then there is a more subtle contrast of Norman Rockwell who demonstrated slices of life in America so well through his art that the United States chamber of commerce in Washington D.C. said, "Through the magic of your talent, the folks next door—their gentle sorrows, their modest joys—have enriched our own lives and given us new insight into our countrymen." (All three demonstrated their abilities to make the world a better place in three very different ways.)

Some patterns with "Nines" might include:

LIFE PATH 9 — THE HUMANITARIAN

Personality Theme: A better world.

Role: Faith. Commitment.

Best at: Breaking ground where few others have the compassion to.

Challenge(s): Balancing needs for physical rewards with spiritual. Can be too focused on dreams and when not achieved can detach and may even blame others (feels victimized).

F.I.P.S.S. (FINANCIAL, INTELLECTUAL, PHYSICAL, SOCIAL, SPIRITUAL):

F—Strong when embrace the idea that material possessions are as much acquired (lucky investments, inheritances, others inspired by your work…) as made, while balancing the idea that work is necessary to live (finding strategic loopholes to help your life flow with ease).

I—Strong when can focus on social impact and harmony. Great as interior and exterior design, socially conscious judge, minister, teacher, lawyer, environmentalist.

P—Strong when achieve overall fitness, which can be a mood balancer/ mind quieter (important when struggle with uncertainty and moodiness that pull you down).

So—Strong when can be connected with variety of diverse people/ situations. Tend to be less judgmental when achieve balance. Being too clingy to people and things can be a challenge.

Sp—Strong when can express philanthropist nature fully. May have additional connection with outdoors and animals.

Famous 9's: Hattie Caraway (first woman elected to U.S. senate), Janet Flanner (journalist, early day environmentalist, awarded French Legion of Honor), Mohandas Gandhi (lawyer, peace activist), Lena Horne (African American singer in early twentieth century), Elvis Presley (singer), Norman Rockwell (slice of life artist), John D. Rockefeller, Sr. (richest man in America during his time), Gloria Steinem (writer, leader in women's equality movement), First Lady—Margaret Taylor, U.S. President and First Lady—Jimmy and Rosalyn Carter, U.S. Presidents—James Buchanan, Rutherford Hayes, William H. Taft.

#11—The In-the-Moment Intuitive... "I see."

"It is the heart always that sees, before the head can see."
                                        —*Thomas Carlyle, Chartism (1839), 5*

"Eleven" is a master number. The double digit master numbers are said to hold more intensity (particularly "11, 22," and "33") than other numbers and takes patience to integrate into a physical life (patience for "Elevens" and for the people who come in contact with them). Life Path "Seven" and "Eleven" combined are dominated by U.S. First Ladies (fourteen total—eight for Life Path "Seven" and six for Life Path "Eleven") in contrast to the U.S. Presidents (ten total—five for Life Path "Seven" and five for Life Path "Eleven").

This can also be called an "Eleven/Two." "Elevens" will have similar qualities to a "Two" Life Path but turbo charged for higher performance and potential lifetime accomplishments. U.S. Presidents include John Adams (helped draft the Declaration of Independence), William (Bill) Clinton, Herbert Hoover (First Lady was master number "Seven"), Franklin Pierce, and Ronald Reagan. U.S. First Ladies included: Abigail Adams (Adams' were Turbo Master Number Couple), Frances Cleveland, Grace Coolidge (Calvin was a "Two" and she was the turbo of the mix), Jackie Kennedy (J. F. Kennedy was master number "Seven"), Dolley Madison, and Martha Washington.

Twenty years were overseen by "Eleven/Two's" in the twentieth and twenty-first centuries (twenty years or nineteen percent served since 1901—one-hundred seven years thru 2008). Adding in First Lady influences (eight more years) would bring the Oval Office to twenty-six percent. These individuals have heightened sensitivity and vision. While very capable of leading, they would have a softer, more charming way of leading (but not quite as low key as a pure "Two"). They are more likely to allow others to take bows for jobs well done and step out of the lime light (many times using this as a partnering or motivational tool). These individuals are the people who are likely to leave the last bit of milk or cookie for others.

But take the everyday person, Rosa Parks, known by many as the Mother of the Civil Rights Movement, who made history by simply saying "no" to the bus driver when he demanded she give up her seat for a white man. One action created a whirlwind of support and civil right activism. A day in the life on December 1, 1955 and a fourteen dollar fine began a city-wide boycott of the bus companies with the goal to desegregate public transportation in the city. A young minister, Martin Luther King, got involved and the boycott went on for over a year, becoming the largest boycott in American history. On December 21, 1956, the Supreme Court ruled that segregation on city buses was unconstitutional. You don't have to be in the Oval Office to have an impact.

The patterns of this dynamic master number "Eleven" can include:

LIFE PATH 11 — THE IN-THE-MOMENT INTUITIVE
Personality Theme: Maximizing the journey and life experiences (highly charged "2").
Role: Seer or visionary.
Best at: Inventing in the moment (as life flows). Leading intuitively.
Challenge(s): Grounding and being practical with matters in the physical.
F.I.P.S.S. (FINANCIAL, INTELLECTUAL, PHYSICAL, SOCIAL, SPIRITUAL):
F—Strong when overcome being impractical. Need focus to realize

full potential. Great inventors, artists, religious leaders, and/or massage, counseling, acupuncture, physical therapy.

I—Strong when confidence is high—very psychic and may not trust that. Likely to expand more with life experiences rather than formal education. Can be very critical of self.

P—Strong when able to balance diet and peaceful environment as an overall lifestyle and protect self from sensory overload from intuitive information.

So—Strong when can overcome withdrawn (at times perceived arrogant) nature as result of receiving intuitive messages. Perceptive to life partners' and others' needs.

Sp—Strong when physically mature (by 30's to 40's) can handle information receiving over and above the obvious senses and connect with a higher source. May be seen as psychic.

Famous 11's: Julie Andrews (singer, actress, children's rights activist, author), Peter Hurkos (world-known psychic detective), Wolfgang Mozart (classical music composer), Rosa Parks (Mother of Civil Rights movement), U.S. First Ladies—Abigail Adams (Adams' were Turbo Master Number couple), Frances Cleveland, Grace Coolidge, Jacqueline Kennedy-Onassis (JFK was "Seven"), Dolley Madison, and Martha Washington, U.S. Presidents—John Adams (helped draft the Declaration of Independence), William (Bill) Clinton, Herbert Hoover, Franklin Pierce, and Ronald Reagan, Charles Windsor—Prince of Wales (heir to the throne of England).

#22—The Material and Humanity Master... "Making my marks."

"The thinker dies, but his thoughts are beyond the reach of destruction. (Wo)men are mortal; but ideas are immortal."
—*Walter Lippmann, A Preface To Morals (1929), 1.3.2*

This would be considered a turbo-charged methodical "Four," with insights of the "Eleven" and is the most powerful physical and spiritual manifester number. This particular Life Path could drive one to exhaustion (and any who come in contact with the "Twenty-two"). They not only have the potential to master the material but also the spiritual/humane. The most ambitious dreams can be manifested into reality with this energy and it is done practically.

The U.S. Oval Office has not been the optimal place for the "Twenty-two" Life Path. Two U.S. Presidents—John Tyler and Andrew Johnson, and interestingly two admired and loved First Ladies of the twentieth century Barbara Bush and Mamie Eisenhower, were part of this group equating to twelve years of influence in the twentieth and twenty-first centuries or eleven percent. But adding together the Life Paths "Five," "Six," "Seven," "Eleven," and "Twenty-two" (if both First Lady and President had a "power number" then the term was only counted once), the U.S. Oval Office had approximately eighty-nine years or eighty-three percent of the past one-hundred and seven years (through 2008) with this cosmic power mix.

While "Twenty-two" is not the optimal Life Path number for the Oval Office to date, these numbers are more effectively found in a diverse people like Mark Twain (author of classics like *Huckleberry Finn*) and the Dalai Lama to name a couple.

The 14th Dalai Lama is the head of state and spiritual leader of the Tibetan people. He was born to a peasant family and was recognized at the age of two, in accordance with Tibetan tradition, as the reincarnation of the 13th Dalai Lama. He is considered (among many other titles) the Buddha of Compassion to his people. He is admired and followed by many in the East and West as a great spiritual leader, has authored many books and does lectures all over the world.

The "Twenty-two" patterns are:

LIFE PATH 22 — THE MATERIAL AND HUMANITY MASTER

Personality Theme: Achieve ultimate financial and spiritual dreams (highly charged "Four"/insightful "11").

Role: Committed to balance. Ambitious. Insightful. Methodical.

Best at: Breaking ground where no others could. Self-confident.

Challenge(s): Resting and taking a back seat to the constant opportunities and projects that present themselves.

F.I.P.S.S. (FINANCIAL, INTELLECTUAL, PHYSICAL, SOCIAL, SPIRITUAL):

F—Strong when create method around insight to manifest dreams. Can over-extend energy and waste time chasing too many opportunities. Focus is key to manifestation.

I—Strong when have enough formal and informal training to fulfill dreams and express visions.

P—Strong when health doesn't take a back seat to material mastery. Stress biggest challenge.

So—Strong when others can keep step with you (and not be intimidated) as you fulfill dreams.

Sp—Strong when surrender to the larger causes and are flexible as new information is introduced. Relaxing will increase internal peace.

Famous 22's: Dalai Lama (14th), Mark Twain (author), First Ladies—Mamie Eisenhower and Barbara Bush, U.S. Presidents—John Tyler and Andrew Johnson.

#33—THE SPIRITUAL TEACHER... "GOTTA HAVE FAITH."

"Not truth, but Faith, it is/That keeps the world alive."
—*Edna St. Vincent Millay, Interim, Renascence (1917)*

This would be a turbo-charged "Six" with a combination of insightful "Eleven" and manifesting "Twenty-two" less the ego. When Jesus Christ was in his early thirties he aggressively pursued a path of teaching the masses. You may have noticed in yourself and others that once reaching thirty, our consciousness seems to shift.

So who has filled the "Thirty-three" shoes? The famous faces haven't revealed themselves to me yet. I'll let you know when I find one. Until then, "Thirty-three" patterns are:

LIFE PATH 33 — THE SPIRITUAL TEACHER

Personality Theme: Spiritually uplifting to (wo)mankind (highly charged server "6"/insightful "11"/manifesting "22").

Role: Devotion. Seeker of understanding and wisdom. Judgment free.

Best at: Strong spiritual influence. Compassion.

Challenge(s): Interfering and enabling rather than helping.

F.I.P.S.S. (FINANCIAL, INTELLECTUAL, PHYSICAL, SOCIAL, SPIRITUAL):

F—Strong when develop reliable tools to help others and can utilize personal charm and charisma to achieve balance and harmony without negative ego.

I—Strong when balanced and connected to self expansion to share with others.

P—Strong when control cravings for dairy and sweets. Generally graceful and attractive.

So—Strong when express balance/counseling side functionally versus controlling. Adored so appropriately accept love in return.

Sp—Strong when taking that savior weight off your shoulders and thrive on spiritual returns as a result of kindness and generosity.

Famous 33's: Rare. See Life Path "Six," "Eleven" and "Twenty-two" for like-personalities.

Astrology Sun Sign Influences

Astrology in its simplest terms is taking a snapshot of the position of the planets connected with the Earth on your birthdate (which can include the exact time of day and place for more intricate processing) to understand your personality patterns, life themes, future and more. There are endless pieces of information that you can extrapolate through Astrology but we will only focus on the strongest planet in our solar system, the one that all planets revolve around and our biggest personality influence—the sun.

Notice that we begin with March (around Spring Equinox). While we have a line in the sand called the new calendar year, spring is actually the mark of new beginnings in relation to the Earth. We'll have a better understanding of how the Sun Sign influences history by:

- Identifying people who have gone down in history who are associated with each Sun Sign
- Sharing a short story about an accomplished person to further demonstrate the personality pattern

- Summarizing the patterns of each Sun Sign so that you might be able to use these to identify your own patterns as well as others'

ARIES—THE CHARMING ACHIEVER… "I DID IT MY WAY."

"It's absurd to divide people into good and bad. People are either charming or tedious."

—Oscar Wilde, Lady Windermere's Fan (1892)

Being first to an Aries doesn't simply mean to lead but also to be recognized and admired while doing so. Talent can run very deep with this Sun Sign which can hinder focus because things can come easy to them. It's important that the Aries commits to some type of specialty (with focus comes credibility and ability to inspire, gain respect and lead).

Aries has not been a dominant Sun Sign for the U.S. Oval Office. In fact, only two U.S. Presidents—Thomas Jefferson, John Tyler and two First Ladies—Elizabeth "Betty" Ford, Lucretia Garfield (did not serve), Lou Hoover were connected to this Sun Sign. But outside of the White House we see accomplished, diverse, independent leaders in a variety of expertise—Leonardo Da Vinci, Sir Elton John, and Sandra Day O'Connor.

The first woman U.S. Supreme Court Justice, Sandra Day O'Connor, was an Aries (as well as a Life Path "Six"). Connor grew up on a 198,000 acre cattle ranch but was more inspired by the big city. Graduating from Stanford Law School, she became assistant attorney general in Arizona in the 1960's. She later became a trial judge and then was appointed to the Arizona Court of Appeals. In 1981 (nominated by Ronald Reagan) she became the U.S. Supreme Court's 102nd justice and its first female member.

Firey Aries traits would be:

ARIES (RAM) ~ MARCH 21ˢᵗ–APRIL 20ᵀᴴ ~ THE CHARMING ACHIEVER

Personality Theme: To be admirably first.

Role: Inspiring leader.

Best at: Being assertive. Generating ideas. Moving on impulse/intuition.

Challenge(s): Changing on the Aries terms. Being temperamental and curt. Focused and specialized.

F.I.P.S.S. (FINANCIAL, INTELLECTUAL, PHYSICAL, SOCIAL, SPIRITUAL):

F—Strong when control impulsive behavior. Can make money, but holding onto can be difficult.

I—Strong when structured enough to become an expert or specialist.

P—Strong when decreases leaping before looking and slows down (focus on one process for health regimen).

So—Strong when perceives being in front. Stronger when values others' ideas/thoughts.

Sp—Strong when not perceived being forced into an idea or told what to do.

Famous Aries: Sandra Day O'Connor (first woman U.S. Supreme Court Justice), Leonardo Da Vinci (painter, inventor, genius visionary), Sir Elton John (musician), Eddie Murphy (actor, comedian), Vincent Van Gogh (artist), Gloria Steinem (writer, leader in women's equality movement), U.S. First Ladies—Elizabeth "Betty" Ford, Lucretia Garfield (did not serve), Lou Hoover, U.S. Presidents—Thomas Jefferson, John Tyler.

TAURUS—THE STABILIZER...
"KEEP YOUR COOL."

"When we are unable to find tranquility within ourselves, it is useless to seek it elsewhere."

—*La Rochefoucauld, Maxims (1665), TR. Kenneth Pratt*

Our U.S. Taurus Oval Office couple are the Buchanans from the mid 1800's. Four U.S. Presidents—James Buchanan, Ulysses S. Grant, James Monroe, Harry Truman, and four U.S. First Ladies—Harriet Lane Buchanan, Dolley Madison (cusp Gemini), Julia Tyler, and Ellen Wilson were primarily in office before the 1900's. Only one of these individuals reigned in the twentieth century—Harry Truman. However, this calming force combined with Life Path "Five" drive is one that has made history in human rights, Coretta Scott King, and has aspired to and achieved balance in the most difficult situations.

Coretta Scott King is the founding president of The King Center in Atlanta, Georgia. She emerged as a national African-American leader after the death of her husband, Martin Luther King, Jr. in the spring of 1968. She has a long resume of accomplishments which include (but aren't limited to), in the mid-1960s, Coretta King's "freedom concerts" demonstrating the history of the civil rights movement. Prior to her husband's passing, she maintained speaking commitments that her husband could not attend (similar to successful U.S. President/First Lady partnerships). After the assassination of Martin Luther King, Jr., Coretta King devoted her life to actively promoting the philosophy of nonviolence. Less than a week after her husband's assassination she led a march on behalf of sanitation workers in Memphis in place of her husband. Only a few weeks following this event, she kept his speaking engagement at an anti-Vietnam war rally in New York. And the next month she helped launch the march on Washington of the Poor People's Campaign. Mrs. King published her autobiography, *My Life with Martin Luther King, Jr.* the following year. But it hasn't stopped there as Mrs. King continues to deliver speeches and write nationally syndicated newspaper columns. Today, with her help, the U.S.A. established a national holiday in honor of Martin Luther King, Jr. and in 1984, was elected chairperson of the Martin Luther King, Jr. Federal Holiday Commission (established by Congress).

Some Taurus traits may include:

TAURUS (BULL) ~ APRIL 20TH–MAY 21ST ~ THE STABILIZER

Personality Theme: The calm in the midst of any storm. Achieves good homes, friends, jobs, marriages, children.

Role: Always there for you. Secure and stable (less impulsive).

Best at: Being there for long-term.

Challenge(s): Being lazy, too comfortable, or complacent.

F.I.P.S.S. (FINANCIAL, INTELLECTUAL, PHYSICAL, SOCIAL, SPIRITUAL):

F—Strong when overcome need to hoard money and Earthly possessions. One of the reasons why great providers, is seek long-term stability.

I—Strong when near (comfortable) home (or what feels like home) on a regular basis.

P—Strong when beat habit of gaining weight (comfort food). Important to keep balanced foods, drinks… as lifestyle.

So—Strong when secure and comfortable.

Sp—Strong when achieves harmony with Earth (this signs element) and spirit.

Famous Taurus: Billy Joel (musician, songwriter), Coretta Scott King (civil rights leader, Martin Luther King's widow), Pope John Paul II (Catholic Pope), Peter Tchaikovsky (classical music composer), U.S. Presidents—James Buchanan, Ulysses S. Grant, James Monroe, Harry Truman, U.S. First Ladies—Harriet Lane Buchanan, Dolley Madison (cusp Gemini), Julia Tyler, Ellen Wilson, Stevie Wonder (musician, songwriter, overcame blindness).

GEMINI—THE WITTY CHANGE AGENT…
"THE ONLY THING THAT'S CONSTANT IS CHANGE."

"You cannot step twice into the same river, for other waters are continually flowing in."
—Heraclitus, "Fragments" (C. 500 B.C.), 21, TR. Philip
Wheelwright

America's first Gemini couple is George H.W. and Barbara Bush but this hasn't been an active Sun Sign for the Oval Office in the twentieth century. Five First Ladies (but one didn't serve and another was on the cusp*) included Barbara Bush, Rachel Jackson (never served), Dolley Madison (Taurus/Gemini cusp), Ida McKinley, Helen Taft, Martha Washington. Two U.S. Presidents—George H. W. Bush and John F. Kennedy were twentieth century office holders as well but JFK was in office for only a short time before he was assassinated.

Witty was not what cosmic America has been seeking in office as a general rule, but it served Mary Cassatt well. Also a Life Path "Eight,"

---

*"Cusp" means that the date that is the beginning point for one Sun Sign is also the ending point for another.

she was brave and aggressive enough to find the means to create the art she loved as well as support herself. Mary Cassatt was born and raised in Philadelphia, PA in a time when women were trained to be good wives and mothers. She would have none of this and enrolled in the local art academy but found them to be too slow and patronizing to women so she moved to Europe to receive private lessons in Paris. A number of her paintings were accepted into the Paris Salon (symbolizing that she was making it as an artist). While she had many setbacks, she became known for out-of-the-box creations—her paintings of women and children were "refreshingly different" according to a *Newsweek* reporter. She found the Impressionistic art style to be pleasing to her for some time and is well known for this but she was always looking for new inspiration. Eleven years before she crossed over, like a cruel joke, she lost her eye sight due to diabetes and was forced to stop painting. While her talent is obvious to observers nearly eighty years after her passing, Cassatt thought her paintings were inadequate. She was quoted as saying near the end of her life, "I have not done what I wanted to... but I tried to make a good fight."

Witty Gemini patterns could include:

GEMINI (TWINS) ~ MAY 21ST–JUNE 22ND ~ THE WITTY CHANGE AGENT

Personality Theme: Trying new things. Being clever—communicating strategically yet artistically.

Role: Communicating like it's an art form. Make out of the box changes because can.

Best at: Being clever, witty communicators.

Challenge(s): Staying interested in anything or anyone long-term. Slowing down and being in the moment. Balancing moods.

F.I.P.S.S. (FINANCIAL, INTELLECTUAL, PHYSICAL, SOCIAL, SPIRITUAL):

F—Strong when balance bank account/budget. Tend to be interested in new technology, ideas, products.

I—Strong when can explore, play with, experience many new technology options, events happening, developments, ideas, places.

P—Strong when can decrease mind noise through physical movement.

So—Strong when overcomes fickle nature for more long-term, inner circle relationships to develop (have many acquaintances).

Sp—Strong when not boring.

Famous Gemini: Mary Cassatt (Impressionist painter), Anne Frank (young writer of Diary of Anne Frank), Marilyn Monroe (actress), Dr. Sally Ride (first American woman in space to orbit Earth), Jeanette Rankin (first woman elected to U.S. Congress), Donald Trump (entrepreneur, real estate developer), John (the Duke) Wayne (actor—witty cowboy, cop, tough guy), U.S. First Ladies— Barbara Bush, Rachel Jackson (never served), Dolley Madison (Taurus/Gemini cusp), Ida McKinley, Helen Taft, Martha Washington, U.S. Presidents—George H. W. Bush, John F. Kennedy.

CANCER—THE COMFORTER...
"HUSH LITTLE BABY DON'T SAY A WORD."

"The important thing is being capable of emotions, but to experience only one's own would be a sorry limitation."
—*Andre Gide, Journals, May 12, 1892, TR. Justin O'Brien*

These are the Cosmic Mothers and Fathers of the world. Not surprising, with Life Path "Sixes" being such a strong influence on the Oval Office. A similar Sun Sign energy, Cancer, has a stronger cosmic pull in the twentieth and twenty-first centuries (seventeen years for Presidents and eight for First

Ladies—twenty-five years or twenty-three percent of one-hundred and seven years — 1901 thru 2008). Four U.S. Presidents—John Quincy Adams, George W. Bush, Calvin Coolidge, Gerald Ford and three U.S. First Ladies—Francis Cleveland, Elizabeth Monroe, and Nancy Reagan are "comforters."

One of the most empathetic icons in the world is Lady Diana Spencer, Princess of Wales. My husband and I were actually in Paris the day that Princess Diana was killed and (we and) Europe were in a state of disbelief. She had an out-of-the-box approach to being a royal. It took a great deal of courage to end her marriage to the heir to the throne, take her story public and even publicly challenge her ex-husband's capability to be the next King. She was dedicated to charities to help children, the homeless and AIDS sufferers. She was the picture of "Cosmic Mother."

Cancer traits could be as follows:

CANCER (CRAB) ~ JUNE 22ND–JULY 23RD ~ THE COMFORTER

Personality Theme: Cosmic Mothers and Fathers.

Role: Nurturers. Empathizers.

Best at: Being dependable. Being intuitive and sensitive to change and (as a result) being great visionaries.

Challenge(s): Smothering those they care about. Hanging on too tightly to events, people, things (including money). Showing their true emotions.

F.I.P.S.S. (FINANCIAL, INTELLECTUAL, PHYSICAL, SOCIAL, SPIRITUAL):

F—Strong when using empathy skills, and can be cutting edge on any front as a result. Rarely without money as have tendency to hold tightly to money.

I—Strong when have someone in life to share knowledge, travel, expansion with.

P—Strong when limit comfort food. Must notice how feel when eat certain products.

So—Strong when nurturing but can form dependence if too nurturing and create opposite effect of people avoiding Cancers.

Sp—Strong when comforted and nurtured.

Famous Cancers: Mary Calderone (Planned Parenthood director, sex expert), Lena Horne (African American singer in early twentieth century), Lady Diana Spencer (Princess of Wales), John Glenn (first astronaut on the moon, Congressman), Helen Keller (blind/deaf author/apeaker/ mentor), John D. Rockefeller, Sr. (richest man in America during his time), U.S. First Ladies—Francis Cleveland, Elizabeth Monroe, Nancy Reagan, U.S. Presidents—John Quincy Adams, George W. Bush, Calvin Coolidge, Gerald Ford.

LEO—THE LEADER OF THE PRIDE...
"EVERYONE STAY TOGETHER."

"We probably have a greater love for those we support than those who support us. Our vanity carries more weight than our self interest."
—*Eric Hoffer, The Passionate State of Mind (1954), 202*

U.S. Presidents—William "Bill" Clinton, Benjamin Harrison, Herbert Hoover, and U.S. First Ladies—Rosalyn Carter, Florence Harding, Anna Harrison, Jacqueline Bouvier Kennedy, and Edith Roosevelt are Leo's. In the twentieth and twenty-first centuries Leo Presidents oversaw the country for twelve years and First Ladies fourteen. So twenty-six years of one-hundred and seven or twenty-four percent were Leo influenced. Again, a more nurturing or

generous sign (while not always perceived this way due to other Leo qualities), this connection has a similar cosmic energy as Cancers and Life Path
"Sixes" in the highest office in America and is the defined Leo "pride"—
in essence, a very large inner circle. Those who have served effectively in
the United States (or, at least, were voted in the office on that perception)
seem to take a great deal of ownership and deeply care for the country.
So the twentieth century would seem to be the age of caring and nurturing in the Oval Office. A woman who eventually went on to nurture the
advancement of women in America, Maria Mitchell, is a great example
of taking care of her defined pride or circle.

Maria Mitchell had many firsts—the first to discover a comet with
the use of a telescope, the first woman admitted to the American Academy
of Arts and Sciences, as well as the American Philosophical Society, a
professor of astronomy at Vassar, the first American woman astronomer,
the first woman elected to the American Academy of Arts and Sciences, the
American Association for the Advancement of Science, and the American
Philosophical Society. A crater on the moon was even named for her (talk
about shining). A Leo overseeing her circle, Mitchell founded and was
president of the American Association for the Advancement of Women.

Leo patterns may include:

Leo (Lion) ~ July 23ʳᵈ–August 22ⁿᵈ ~ The Leader of the Pride

Personality Theme: Being in the spotlight. Establishing a pride/
group/circle.

Role: To take care of the pride (circle of friends/family). To lead
and shine.

Best at: Outward self-expression, creativity and willpower.

Challenge(s): Being self-absorbed. Being overly generous as result of
taking care of the "pride" (circle of friends/family).

F.I.P.S.S. (FINANCIAL, INTELLECTUAL, PHYSICAL, SOCIAL, SPIRITUAL):

F—Strong when image is not ruler. Balance physical expression with realistic financial situation.

I—Strong when personal image is healthy, and no limits to expanding knowledge.

P—Strong when temptation to be lazy doesn't take over. Usually very healthy (connected with image).

So—Strong when doesn't expect a lot in return for generosity. Try not to keep score.

Sp—Strong when limelight is less important than connecting to spirit.

Famous Leos: Emperor Napoleon Bonaparte (French military leader), Elizabeth Dole (senator, 2000 U.S. Presidential hopeful/never ran), Amelia Earhart (first woman pilot to cross the Atlantic solo), Arnold Schwarzenegger (weightlifter, actor, politician), U.S. Presidents—William "Bill" Clinton, Benjamin Harrison, Herbert Hoover, U.S. First Ladies—Rosalyn Carter, Florence Harding, Anna Harrison, Jacqueline Bouvier Kennedy, Edith Roosevelt.

VIRGO—THE DETAILED CONSTANT EXPANDER... "WHEN YOU WANT SOMETHING DONE RIGHT..."

"Some people like to make a little garden out of life and walk down a path."

—*Jean Anouilh, The Lark, (1955), 2, Adapted by Lillian Hellman*

The majority of Virgos in the White House to date seemed to be out of sync. Lyndon Johnson was known for being bossy and critical in public with his wife (showing disrespect for the feminine balance). Taft wanted to be a Supreme Court Justice instead of President but his wife pushed him into the White House. A couple of the First Ladies were absentee (physically or just didn't want to be there). Two others were known for banning drinking, smoking and/or card playing (not a very popular thing to do in the 1800's). These U.S. Presidents— Lyndon Johnson, William H. Taft and U.S. First Ladies—Ellen Arthur (never served), Lucy Hayes (banned alcohol from White House), Sarah Polk (banned drinking, smoking and card playing from White House), Margaret Taylor (participated very little in Oval Office) were meant to expand more outside of the White House.

For people like Sean Connery (award-winning actor), Michael Jackson (award-winning singer, songwriter), and Stephen King (author) the details have made all the difference to their extra-ordinary successes. This includes the detailed that teach the detailed.

Maria Montessori was a ground breaking activist, educator and healer born in Italy. She created the Montessori approach to teaching and it has been adopted all over the world as a gold standard. She was not about to be told "no" (the Life Path "One" in her) and was the first woman in Italy to receive a degree of Doctor of Medicine (1896). She became an outstanding and respected speaker and, among many other causes, fought for working women and against the exploitation of child labor. As a Doctor she was able to observe mentally challenged children and some of those simple observations translated to applying learning principles to children with normal learning patterns as well. This ground-breaking process allowed children the freedom to learn at their specific development levels which included accelerated learning.

Some of the traits that might be found in Virgos are:

VIRGO (VIRGIN) ~ AUGUST 22ND–SEPTEMBER 22ND ~ THE DETAILED CONSTANT EXPANDER.

Personality Theme: Serving the greater good. Seeking detailed order. Constant self-improvement.

Role: Worker bee. Organizer and analyzer (on own detailed terms).

Best at: Organizing, analyzing and efficiently fixing things on own detailed terms (know where everything is, even when observers perceive disorganization).

Challenge(s): Letting the mind, body and spirit relax in the moment as opposed to constantly improving and analyzing the details.

F.I.P.S.S. (FINANCIAL, INTELLECTUAL, PHYSICAL, SOCIAL, SPIRITUAL):

F—Strong when can improve, dig into details and be the influencer of the outcome.

I—Strong when studies/travel allows practical expansion.

P—Strong when decrease stress of being too detailed. Tend to need clear benefits of what is truly healthy in order to fully embrace.

So—Strong when move past the idea that all relationships have to be perfect and allow for play time.

Sp—Strong when enough information is gathered that points to being on the best path. Some have a major connection to Earth and plants (particularly those that have a clear purpose, like healing).

Famous Virgos: Sir Sean Connery (actor), Michael Jackson (singer, songwriter), Stephen King (author), Maria Montessori (educator and creator of Montessori education process), U.S. Presidents—Lyndon Johnson, William H. Taft, U.S. First Ladies— Ellen Arthur (never served), Lucy Hayes, Sarah Polk, Margaret Taylor (participated very little in Oval Office).

LIBRA—THE BALANCER... "ON ONE HAND... ON THE OTHER HAND... "

"To be always ready a (wo)man must be ready to cut a knot, for everything cannot be untied."
—*Henri Frederic Amiel, JOURNAL, June 16, 1851, TR. Mrs. Humphrey Ward*

Libra's have a tendency to take a look at more than one perspective and sometimes there is no end to this, simply more questions. On the other hand, if there are First Born, or Middle child tendencies (found in most of the Presidents and First Ladies) with Life Path "Power Numbers" ("Five," "Six," "Seven," "Eleven," or "Twenty-two"), it could be a positive to take a closer look at a variety of opinions but still have the capability to make a decision. U.S. Presidents—Chester Arthur (inherited the office), Jimmy Carter, Dwight Eisenhower, Rutherford Hayes and First Ladies—Caroline Harrison, Martha Jefferson (never served), Eliza Johnson, Anna Roosevelt, Edith Wilson were balancers. So, the balance was more powerful when adding Mr. Eisenhower's Oval Office effective, Life Path "Six" (8 years in office), First Ladies Wilson's "Seven" (for 6 years) and Anna Roosevelt's "Six" (for 8 years). Twenty-six years in the twentieth and twenty-first centuries were overseen by Libras or twenty-four percent of the period 1901 through 2008. So in Libra style, it's about looking at more than one variable to come to the optimal answer.

A picture of balance and classic beauty is Julie Andrews (also a Life Path "Eleven"). She fulfilled her Sun Sign dream at a very early age as she grew up in the entertainment world with her parents. She traveled a great deal and made her stage debut by age twelve (had singing lessons as early as eight). She became the youngest person to ever perform in front of English royalty and continued on to do classics like *The Sound of Music*, *Mary Poppins* and many other hit films. By the 1970's she began publishing children's books under the name Julie Edwards. Mrs. Andrews is mother to five children and adopted two other children in the 1970's. In Libra style she gives back to bring balance to her charmed life by supporting and promoting a number of charities, including Operation USA, UNICEF and Save the Children. She also served as Goodwill Ambassador for UNIFEM in the 1990's.

LIBRA (SCALES) ~ SEPTEMBER 22ND–OCTOBER 23RD ~ THE BALANCER

Personality Theme: Strives for balance in all things.

Role: Joining both sides/halves with the ultimate goal of achieving beauty and harmony.

Best at: Manifesting beauty and balance (often expressed with the arts).

Challenge(s): Being decisive. Unrealistically looking for perfection in all things.

F.I.P.S.S. (FINANCIAL, INTELLECTUAL, PHYSICAL, SOCIAL, SPIRITUAL):

F—Strong when sees immediate return and connection with beauty/harmony/perfection.

I—Strong when able to travel and study the arts.

P—Strong when inner thoughts match outer beauty/perfection (physical surroundings as well as body).

So—Strong when being admired and can share beauty/harmony/perfection vision.

Sp—Strong when is immediately obvious that overall perfection/harmony can be achieved.

Famous Libra: Julie Andrews (singer, actress, children's rights activist, author), Mohandas Gandhi (lawyer, peace activist), Reverend Jesse Jackson (civil rights leader), John Lennon (singer, songwriter, peace advocate), U.S. First Ladies—Caroline Harrison, Martha Jefferson (never served), Eliza Johnson, Anna Roosevelt, Edith Wilson, Frances Willard (educator, reformer), U.S. Presidents—Chester Arthur (inherited the office), Jimmy Carter, Dwight Eisenhower, Rutherford Hayes.

SCORPIO—THE PATIENT ACHIEVER...
"RIGHT TIME, RIGHT PLACE."

"Patience, and the mulberry leaf becomes a silk gown."
—**Chinese Proverb**

The most famous First Scorpio Couple is John (second President) and Abigail Adams. Not only were they both Scorpios but both were Life Path "Eleven/Twos." Truman was quoted as saying, "She (Abigail) would have been a better President than her husband." Only one of the five Presidents bore this Sun Sign in the 1900's and beyond and included U.S. Presidents— John Adams, James Garfield, Warren Harding, James Polk, and Theodore Roosevelt. The twentieth and twenty-first centuries were more dominant for the Scorpio U.S. First Ladies—Abigail Adams, Laura Bush, Hillary Clinton (later becoming U.S. senator), Mamie Eisenhower, Letitia Tyler (sickly and inactive in White House). Only one of the First Ladies was not in the twentieth century and beyond (didn't count Tyler since she was inactive). Presidents and life partners combined, there were thirty-two years of Scorpio's from 1901 through 2008 or thirty percent.

Known to be a quiet, focused Scorpio, Dr. Marie Curie won the Nobel Peace Prize for the advancement of chemistry, discovering the elements radium and polonium. Curie was head of the Physics department at

Sorbonne in 1906 (the first time a woman held this type of position), and was highly respected by her peers. It's no wonder, as she was a member of the Committee of Intellectual Co-operation of the League of Nations, earned her Doctor of Science degree, received numerous honorary degrees and had written a number of books on radioactive substances and other related subjects. Focused until the end, from 1911 until her death she was a member of the Conseil du Physique Solvay.

Qualities that you might find in a Scorpio are as follows:

SCORPIO (SCORPION) ~ OCTOBER 23RD–NOVEMBER 22ND ~ THE PATIENT ACHIEVER

Personality Theme: Keeping everything and everyone in line.

Role: In control.

Best at: Being patient while inwardly maintaining passion and commitment.

Challenge(s): Sharing feelings — can be very intense and need a lot of space when processing. Feelings get hurt easily as well.

F.I.P.S.S. (FINANCIAL, INTELLECTUAL, PHYSICAL, SOCIAL, SPIRITUAL):

F—Strong when given opportunity, excels with any job. Savers of money.

I—Strong when phenomena or puzzles to be solved, or concepts to be molded (how did they build that? How can that be rethought?...).

P—Strong when let go of anger/resentments (sometimes builds to revenge). Must achieve to be fully physically well.

So—Strong when overcome need to be alone because hiding feelings and overcome need to have everyone in line to your satisfaction.

Sp—Strong when embrace the concept of faith and see value in being happy.

Famous Scorpions: Dr. Marie Curie (Nobel Peace Prize in advancement of chemistry), Jodie Foster (actress, film director), Bill Gates (MicroSoft founder), Princess Grace (Kelly) of Monaco, Robert Kennedy (former U.S. senator), Charles Windsor, Prince of Wales (heir to the throne of England), U.S. First Ladies—Abigail Adams, Laura Bush, Hillary Clinton (later becoming U.S. senator), Mamie Eisenhower, Letitia Tyler (sickly and inactive in White House), U.S. Presidents—John Adams, James Garfield, Warren Harding, James Polk, Theodore Roosevelt.

SAGITTARIUS—THE LIFE PARTAKER... "GIVE HER FREEDOM OR GIVE HER DEATH."

"Freedom is one of the principal goals of human endeavor, but the best use man can make of his freedom is to place limitation upon it."
—*Edwin Grant Conklin, Science And The Faith*
Of The Modern, Scribners Magazine, 1925

There was only one Sag in the U.S. Oval Office in the twentieth and twenty-first centuries (one First Lady). The U.S. Presidents—Franklin Pierce (wife not supportive, lost all three sons), Zachary Taylor (died in office), Martin Van Buren (known for being non-committal and lost re-election)—didn't have very positive experiences while in office. The U.S. First Ladies had equally challenging Oval Office experiences—Claudia Johnson (criticized by husband publicly), and Mary Lincoln (tragic life). These individuals' experiences ranged from major disappointments on the job to the loss of children and spouses, and death in office.

Emily Dickinson was an American Lyrical Poet with only seven of her approximately 1800 poems published in her lifetime. It's reported that she was quite social until she was about twenty-three years old. Then she was known to be an extremely private person which is very uncommon for a Sagittarian. Possibly she perceived she was rejected by the audience that she so desired as a Sag (possibly her work, maybe someone broke her heart, or some other mystery). In any case, she spent the rest of her life in her room expressing her Life Path "Seven" traits of being focused and (unbeknownst to her) an expert, becoming one of the most famous poets of the nineteenth century. (See Life Path "7" section for more details).

This is a small sampling of the world and doesn't mean that Sagittarians are doomed. What it currently shows is U.S. Presidents and First Ladies haven't had a very positive time thus far. What we also know is Sagittarians are fun-loving and being trapped (mentally or physically) is the ultimate torture for this Sun Sign.

Here are some patterns you are likely to see from Sagittarians:

SAGITTARIUS (ARCHER) ~ NOVEMBER 22ND–DECEMBER 22ND ~ THE LIFE PARTAKER

Personality Theme: Combining fun and freedom of the journey to eventually find the meaning of life that unites everyone (or many key people).

Role: Life of the party (of a large admiring audience). Networker— Knows key people.

Best at: Adjusting to changes in scenery and life situations. Idea generation.

Challenge(s): Complete commitment (calming the stallion) and attention to detail.

F.I.P.S.S. (FINANCIAL, INTELLECTUAL, PHYSICAL, SOCIAL, SPIRITUAL):

F—Strong when resources are available (especially others' resources). Growth likely when accompanied by focus.

I—Strong when creative expression allowed.

P—Strong when learn to slow down and focus.

So—Strong when have audience (party people). Over time will enrich life when differentiate party and inner circles.

Sp—Strong when doesn't interfere with freedom.

Famous Sagittarians: Woody Allen (actor, director, writer), Emily Dickinson (American lyrical poet), Walt Disney (artist, creator of Disney cartoons and related properties), Bruce Lee (actor, martial arts expert), Steven Spielberg (movie director), Mark Twain (author of classics like Huckleberry Finn), U.S. First Ladies with less positive Oval Office experiences—Claudia Johnson (criticized by husband publicly), Mary Lincoln (tragic life), U.S. Presidents—Franklin Pierce (wife not supportive, lost all three sons), Zachary Taylor (died in office), Martin Van Buren (known for being non-committal and lost re-election).

CAPRICORN—THE CLIMBER...
"UP, UP, AND AWAY!"

"If your heart is quite set upon a crown, make and put on one of roses, for it will make the prettier appearance."
—*Epictetus, Discourses (2nd c.), 1.19, TR. Thomas W. Higginson*

While we had a number of Capricorn Sun Signs in the Oval Office, what is most prominent are the difficulties experienced. They include, but aren't limited to, two impeachments and one stroke while in office. While Capricorns are known for their ability to become leaders in their fields of choice, the Oval Office hasn't been their optimal workplace to date. U.S. Presidents include Millard Fillmore (inherited office), Andrew Johnson (acquitted impeachment), Richard Nixon (resigned due to impeachment),

Woodrow Wilson (stroke and paralyzed before ending term) and First Lady—Grace Coolidge.

The key is to manage power with experiencing a full, functional, positive life. There are many other Capricorns that have lived long, happy lives like Emily Greene Balch, Nobel Peace Prize recipient, living well into her nineties. And while there are the leaders that passed away early in life, their legacies still burn brightly like Joan of Arc. Some believe that Joan of Arc was a clairvoyant. By the time she was thirteen she was having visions and hearing voices that she believed were from Saints. She was instrumental in helping the King of France drive the English off of French soil. By the time she was seventeen she led the military to victory on a number of occasions driving the English out of France. She was captured by the English and tried as a heretic for saying that the voices and messages she received were from God. After her death, she was declared innocent (following her family insistence of reviewing the evidence) and by the twentieth century she was declared a Saint by the Catholic church.

Some of the patterns that might be indicative of a Capricorn are:

CAPRICORN (GOAT) ~ DECEMBER 22ND–JANUARY TWENTY-FIRST ~ THE CLIMBER

Personality Theme: The "One" in ultimate control and power (of themselves and others).

Role: Ambitious and goal-oriented to build something that will last (stable). Willing to move slowly to reach his/her fullest power potential.

Best at: Manifesting success through slow, organized, calculated methods. Patience. Helping build a situation/society/event that serves the masses. Creating foundation.

Challenge(s): Positively remembering the people that sponsored success and not always linking to power and position. Being okay that it is lonely at the top. Overcoming tendency to be cold, rigid, suspicious.

F.I.P.S.S. (FINANCIAL, INTELLECTUAL, PHYSICAL, SOCIAL, SPIRITUAL):

F—Strong when creates a solid foundation. Reaches the top of many fields and money is (many times) the key to getting there.

I—Strong when study/travel gains leadership/power position.

P—Strong when keep pessimism low so body will not absorb negativity.

So—Strong when consistently loyal to inner circle relationships/past sponsors (tendency to overlook individuals for the masses). Important to manage pride/power need.

Sp—Strong when creates comfort, warmth and security and compatible with leadership goals.

Famous Capricorns: Joan of Arc (martyr, saint), Muhammad Ali (prize fighter), Emily Greene Balch (1946 Nobel Peace Prize winner, economist, social scientist), Martin Luther King Jr. (civil rights leader), Alice Paul (led nineteenth Amendment of the constitution passage/authored Equal Rights Amendment), Elvis Presley (singer), First Lady—Grace Coolidge, U.S. Presidents—Millard Fillmore (inherited office), Andrew Johnson (acquitted impeachment), Richard Nixon (resigned due to impeachment), Woodrow Wilson (stroke and paralyzed before ending term).

AQUARIUS—OUT OF THE BOX...
"DREAM IT AND IT WILL COME."

"Who in Europe could have thought of the disappearing bed, a bed during the night, a handsome wardrobe during the day? Where else (than in the United States) could the rocking chair have been invented, in which a man could move and sit still at the same time?"

—*Luigi Barzini, O America (1977)*

In the twentieth and twenty-first centuries, twenty-eight years were overseen (through 2008) by Aquarians—twenty by Presidents and eight by one First Lady. U.S. Presidents include William Henry Harrison, Abraham Lincoln, William McKinley, Ronald Reagan, Franklin D. Roosevelt and First Ladies were Louisa Adams (John Quincy's wife), Julia Grant, and Elizabeth Truman. These were largely historically positive Oval Office interactions with Ronald Reagan, Franklin D. Roosevelt and Elizabeth Truman (known to be a relied upon confident of her husband). These Oval Office personalities were in good company with innovators like Charles Darwin, Thomas Edison, Charles Lindbergh, Oprah Winfrey, Hattie Caraway and more.

Hattie Caraway was the first woman elected to the U.S. senate (from Arkansas). She was first appointed when her husband died unexpectedly and was re-elected twice. She was nicknamed "Silent Hattie" because she didn't make any speeches on the floor. She built a reputation of integrity through other means and maintained a type of housewife image. She was known to be more of an independent but supported the Roosevelt New Deal, and was a prohibitionist. Even in 1938 when her opponent had a slogan "Arkansas needs another man in the senate," she still won by a sizeable margin (women were allowed to vote by this time). She was not only supported by organizations representing women, but veterans and union members.

Aquarian patterns would be:

Aquarius (Water Bearer) ~ January 21ˢᵀ–February 19ᵀᴴ ~ Out of the Box

Personality Theme: Diverse, out-of-the-box trend detectives and setters.

Role: Open-minded (sometimes considered eccentric) change agents (but stubbornly firm on "different" ideas).

Best at: Manifesting ideas well before their time (not limited to one area of expertise). "Seeing" past self and more toward masses. Being social.

Challenge(s): Being bored and detached. Can be very social but connecting with individuals can sometimes be a chore when consumed with innovating.

F.I.P.S.S. (Financial, Intellectual, Physical, Social, Spiritual):

F—Strong when work with cutting edge (includes arts, sciences...) and manage tendency to overextend in various ways.

I—Strong when able to study creative/out-of-the-box concepts and places.

P—Strong when exercise grounds in the physical and feels like part of this world. Tendency to be attractive and coordinated.

So—Strong when doesn't sacrifice relationships for higher good (can detach to achieve the "good"). Very giving and will open home to anyone for sake of overall humanity. Generally likeable.

Sp—Strong when connecting to the higher good, diversity and overall humanity.

Famous Aquarians: Hattie Caraway (first woman elected to U.S. senate), Charles Darwin (naturalist on evolution and natural selection), Thomas Edison (inventor—light bulb and devices to expand usage, alkaline battery, motion picture camera...), Michael Jordan (basketball star), Charles Lindbergh (record setting pilot), Wolfgang Mozart (classic music composer), Rosa Parks (Mother of Civil Rights movement), Babe Ruth (pro baseball player), Oprah Winfrey (actress, magazine editor, entertainer/talk show host).

PISCES—THE INTUITIVE VISUALIZER...
"FEEL YOUR WAY."

"He does not believe that does not live according to his belief."
—*Thomas Fuller, M.D., Gnomologia (1732), 1838*

This was a Sun Sign that had little influence on the twentieth and twenty-first centuries Oval Office and included U.S. Presidents Grover Cleveland, Andrew Jackson, James Madison, George Washington and First Ladies Abigail Fillmore, Thelma "Pat" Nixon, Jane Pierce, and Hannah Van Buren. However, innovating through intuition has played a major role in the twentieth and twenty-first centuries with inventors like Alexander Graham Bell and Albert Einstein. A woman innovating ahead of her time was Janet Flanner.

Janet Flanner was a skilled intuitive journalist and ahead of her time environmentalist/preservationist in the early 1900's. She was raised in Indiana surrounded by nature and moved to New York City (among other areas) noticing how buildings were replacing nature and driving wildlife away. As a result, she wrote a fictional book called "The Cubical City" that reflected her concerns on the environmental front (including major issues in the twenty-first century of deforestation and urban sprawl). As a journalist she also addressed the many issues connected with the wars of her time and the destruction of history as a result. Recognized as a true visionary, Flanner was one of the few women awarded the French Legion of Honor.

Qualities of Pisces might include:

PISCES (FISHES) ~ FEBRUARY 19ᵀᴴ–MARCH 21ˢᵀ ~ THE INTUITIVE VISUALIZER

Personality Theme: Believing in and understanding others. Having faith.

Role: Intuitive/Heightened Sensitive. Spiritual Motivator and Visualizer.

Best at: Bringing others to higher levels through listening, sympathy and empathy.

Challenge(s): Taking on others' feelings as own. Understanding self. Being realistic.

F.I.P.S.S. (FINANCIAL, INTELLECTUAL, PHYSICAL, SOCIAL, SPIRITUAL):

F—Strong when intuitive hunches are practical and finances are carefully managed. Many prefer behind the scenes work.

I—Strong when study/travel effectively combines dreamy/imaginary and real worlds.

P—Strong when can manage tendency to overindulge. High sensitivity to environment, food, drink, drugs, sugar and bad doses of other people.

So—Strong when have a special physical space to share with inner circle friends. At times prefer to be alone and even hide from the world (especially if hurt by those trusted in past).

Sp—Strong when understands self as much as others, and has faith in own intuition.

Famous Pisces: Alexander Graham Bell (inventor), Albert Einstein (genius, inventor, E=MC²), Janet Flanner (journalist, early day environmentalist/preservationist, awarded French Legion of Honor), Jerry Lewis (actor, philanthropist), Michelangelo (artist), Elizabeth Taylor (actress, philanthropist), U.S. First Ladies—Abigail Fillmore, Thelma "Pat" Nixon, Jane Pierce, Hannah Van Buren, U.S. Presidents—Grover Cleveland, Andrew Jackson, James Madison, George Washington.

Birth Order Influences

It's believed by some experts that we develop our Birth Order personality patterns by age two. Put in unscientific terms, Birth Order is a label each child psychologically owns within a family unit—First born, Only, Middle, or Youngest. Unlike Astrology and Numerology, where most agree on what each Sun Sign, destiny or Life Path number mean, there are a number of theories on the Birth Order concept. I have chosen to embrace the idea that there are no bad Birth Orders, simply opportunities to learn and expand to new levels.

We'll have a better understanding of how each Birth Order influences history by:

- Identifying people who have gone down in history that are associated with each Birth Order
- Sharing a short story about an accomplished person to further demonstrate the personality pattern
- Summarizing the patterns of each Birth Order so that you might be able to use these to identify your own patterns as well as others'

FIRST BORN—THE ACHIEVER...
"LEADING THE WAY."

"The ability to concentrate and to use your time well is everything if you want to succeed in business—or almost anywhere else, for that matter."

—*Lee Iacocca, Iacocca: An Autobiography (1984) with William Novak*

The majority of U.S. Presidents and First Ladies are First Born boys or girls. It seems that those with the number one birth position are simply looking to stay on the top in all areas of life. For your own little experiment, ask people who hold positions of authority from school age up to adulthood about their Birth Orders. Keep score and remember the rules of thumb under the terms section at the beginning of this book.

Hillary Rodham Clinton is a First Born. She was a lawyer by training, the U.S. First Lady for most of the 1990's, and early in her husband's term was known not to take a back seat in the White House. As a result she became unpopular and took it down a notch for the balance of her husband's term to keep the peace. But once her First Lady term was up, she ran and won a seat as U.S. Senator. You can't keep a First down!

First Born children might demonstrate the following:

FIRST BORN—THE ACHIEVER

Personality Theme: In control. The one in power.

Role: Ambitious, goal-oriented, conformist, responsible, organized.

Best at: Bringing people, projects, events together on time, following rules.

Challenge(s): Being too controlling and putting pressure on self and others to perform to their expectations.

F.I.P.S.S. (Financial, Intellectual, Physical, Social, Spiritual):

F—Strong when can be precise/detailed but able to think outside of the box to establish new ideas/rules. Prefers to lead.

I—Strong when can collect facts and rules that can be established or followed.

P—Strong when can look like a leader (fit, lean, good looking) but if become too stressed "leading" can wear on the body.

So—Strong when overcome need to be too perfect and too demanding (decreases strain on relationships).

Sp—Strong when makes logical sense, and laws and rules are clear. Important to understand need to lighten up for inner health.

Famous Firsts: Majority of U.S. Presidents and First Ladies, Sir Sean Connery (actor, "James Bond"), Albert Einstein (genius, inventor, $E=MC^2$), William Shakespeare (author).

Only—The Turbo Achiever...
"I did it the only way!"

"The great and glorious masterpiece of man is to know how to live to purpose."
—*Montaigne, Of Experience, Essays (1580-88), TR. W. C. Hazlitt*

Being an Only is the number three Birth Order of U.S. Presidents and First Ladies. While they are turbo achievers, they can be very self-centered. Onlies had to create their own fun and entertainment since they had no siblings growing up (or siblings were much older). As adults, they may continue to be very independent and look out for what's in their best interests, not recognizing others' needs at times.

Lena Horne, an accomplished singer (her signature song is "Stormy

Weather") and activist, was born to an accomplished African American family (said to also have Cherokee Indian and Caucasian bloodlines as well) but their marriage only lasted until she was three-years-old. Her mother was an entertainer and took her on the road a great deal but her most stable home was with her grandparents. As an African American entertainer, she had many challenges and it was even suggested that she try to pass for white or even Latin American to help her career along. She refused. Some of her political affiliations put her on the "red list" and kept her out of the entertainment world for quite some time. To add to her challenges, Lena married a white man (her second marriage) and because of difficulties in America, they decided to move to a more open-minded country at the time, France. She did it her way!

Some Only patterns may include:

ONLY—THE TURBO ACHIEVER

Personality Theme: The Center of the World. Independent Creator.

Role: Goal-oriented, accumulator of knowledge, independent problem solver/creator.

Best at: Planning, setting and reaching goals that clearly benefit the Only.

Challenge(s): Seeing past the "Only" way.

F.I.P.S.S. (FINANCIAL, INTELLECTUAL, PHYSICAL, SOCIAL, SPIRITUAL):

F—Strong when willing to rely on own abilities as opposed to being taken care of by others. Will sacrifice everything to succeed.

I—Strong when can collect facts.

P—Strong when can look like a leader (fit, lean, good looking) but if become too stressed "leading" can wear on the body (addictions can become an issue for escape).

So—Strong when receives attention. Most comfortable with older and younger friends usually. If understand how to put others first then develops more meaningful circles of friends.

Sp—Strong when makes logical sense and demonstrates clear personal benefits to self-fulfillment.

Famous Onlies: Third ranked Birth Order for U.S. Presidents and First Ladies including Bill Clinton (9 year gap between brother) and Franklin D. Roosevelt, Lena Horne (African American singer in beginning early twentieth century), Leonardo da Vinci (painter, inventor, genius visionary), Elizabeth Dole ("Only" but youngest charm, senator, 2000 U.S. Presidential hopeful/never ran)

MIDDLE—THE NEGOTIATOR...
"I'VE GOT TO BE ME."

"It is better to lose the saddle than the horse." —**Italian Proverb**

Being a Middle is the second ranking Birth Order of U.S. Presidents and First Ladies. This makes intuitive sense as negotiating is such a helpful quality when dealing with many personalities. For Princess Grace (Kelly) of Monaco being a passionate Scorpio and driven Life Path "Eight," this paved her way to success as an actress but her skills as a Middle child would be even more crucial when marrying into the royal family of Monaco. She quickly assimilated into the culture and was loved instantly by her new found country. Even after her death she continues to be loved, admired and missed by many.

Middles can be very unpredictable ranging from rebel to pleaser depending on the family dynamics. These can be the more independent children in the household (or, better put, outside of the household) as they will look outside of the family to create a support network. These kids are likely to adopt additional families (visiting others regularly, sleeping over at friends' homes…). They seem more daring as they look to manifest or weave their dreams.

Middle traits could include:

MIDDLE—THE NEGOTIATOR

Personality Theme: Weaving own dreams with realism.

Role: Diplomat, negotiator, risk-taker, competitor (larger family, at times less competitive).

Best at: Compromising. Making friends. Being flexible and cooperative.

Challenge(s): Confrontation (rather please others) but can be rebel, independent, stubborn, and/or secretive (sometimes), competitiveness varies.

F.I.P.S.S. (FINANCIAL, INTELLECTUAL, PHYSICAL, SOCIAL, SPIRITUAL):

F—Strong when balance risk taking and pleaser generosity with creating future security.

I—Strong when focus on a course of study long enough. Life experiences and working with people is high intellectual stimulant.

P—Strong when social circle encourages fitness and/or if gets recognition/seems special.

So—Strong when feel like part of groups, events, clubs, teams. Loyal to friends and commitments but can be secretive and not ask for help if needed.

Sp—Strong when not seen as a way to decrease independent thinking, hold people down or categorize others disrespectfully. Important to fill social need.

Famous Middles: Second ranked Birth Order for U.S. Presidents and First Ladies, Emperor Napoleon Bonaparte (French military leader),

Charles Darwin (naturalist on evolution and natural selection), Princess Grace (Kelly) of Monaco, Donald Trump (entrepreneur, real estate developer)

YOUNGEST—THE CHARMER... "JUST WANNA HAVE FUN."

"Style is a magic wand, and turns everything to gold that it touches."
—*Logan Pearsall Smith, Afterthoughts (1931)*

Being a Youngest child is the least likely Birth Order of U.S. Presidents and First Ladies. While courage, the desire to lead, compete and achieve goals are higher ranked personality traits in the Oval Office, it worked like a charm for Ronald Reagan. Here is where you find the fun-loving bunch. Their challenge is to kick "the baby" wrap so they don't feel like they need to be served all the time.

Here's an interesting mix—an Only in Youngest clothing. With someone like Elizabeth Dole, U.S. senator and (didn't run due to money issues) 2000 U.S. hopeful Presidential candidate, the Leo and Life Path "One" (leader) qualities keep her sharp and in the spotlight. While some would consider her having the Youngest charm, she actually had a brother thirteen years older which makes her an "Only." She held two U.S. cabinet posts in the Reagan (first woman to be head of Department of Transportation) and Bush Senior administrations and was the president of the Red Cross for most of the 1990's (only other woman to hold this position was the founder in 1881). However, she was raised in (polite) North Carolina in the thirties and forties and her mother always hoped that she would grow up, marry a nice man and build a house next to hers (Dole has been quoted as saying her mom is her best friend). Instead she fought against women's and minorities' glass ceilings and earned degrees at Harvard and more. Elizabeth Dole is very (Youngest) charming, and when her husband ran for office she became America's sweetheart giving up her posts twice to support her husband's bid for higher office (very un-Only). She is divinely feminine, wears bright, cheery clothing (as much a Leo quality as Youngest) demonstrating confidence and is perceived as fun-loving. So it just goes to show, baselines are meant to be broken (just thought I'd burst the bubble a bit).

Here are some likely patterns of Youngest children:

YOUNGEST—THE CHARMER

Personality Theme: Enjoy life. Outgoing. Expressive.

Role: Fun, funny, people person, loving and lovable.

Best at: Working with small groups or one-on-one. Creative, innovative thinking since they are more fun-loving, open and feel less pressure to perform.

Challenge(s): Listening. Being grown up. Following rules (question authority).

F.I.P.S.S. (FINANCIAL, INTELLECTUAL, PHYSICAL, SOCIAL, SPIRITUAL):

F—Strong when figure out how to be a grown up and still express creativity and fun personality functionally. Great in sales.

I—Strong when turn natural ability to read people and situations into educational experience (formal education can be a challenge).

P—Strong when figure out how to discipline fun loving nature, food, drink, drugs, and sugar.

So—Strong when not seeking as much attention (natural entertainer) and can find more meaningful, reliable, inner circle.

Sp—Strong when can figure out how to balance being served with serving others.

Famous Youngests: Last ranked Birth Order for U.S. Presidents and First Ladies but includes Ronald Reagan, Thomas Edison (inventor—light bulb and devices to expand usage, alkaline battery, motion picture camera...), Mohandas Gandhi (lawyer, peace activist), Mark Twain (author of classics like *Huckleberry Finn*).

IV.
In the Mix, in-the-Moment

Earth Cycles

As you will also find in my books *Adventures Of A Mainstream Metaphysical Mom* and *"Soul"utions*, the cycles of the Earth influence our short-term abilities to get things done on a day-to-day basis. When observing the cycles of the Earth, our physical and spiritual existence are keenly aware of the Earth shifts. We observe them by responding to the cycle as if we were a plant or animal. The theory is that our bodies are seventy to ninety percent water. What happens to water when seasons shift?

- Spring — renews, supports new life.
- Summer — can evaporate from heat which means molecules are moving faster.
- Winter — molecules slow down and even stop when frozen.
- Fall — the sun shifts, temperature changes and plant life begins to change and/or die, animal life migrates.

Our physical bodies, even if we don't recognize it, are going through similar transitions. If ignored, we get physically sick, have problems achieving goals, and more.

In this section we'll have a better understanding of how each cycle steers our existence by:

- Summarizing the patterns of the cycles so that you might be able to use these to identify your own patterns as well as others'
- Sharing cycle observations so you can adopt the concepts to your daily life

SPRING—NEW BEGINNINGS AND PLANTING... "OPENING TO THE POSSIBILITIES."

"In our hearts those of us who know anything worth knowing know that March a new year begins, and if we plan any new leaves, it will be when the rest of Nature is planning them too."
—*Joseph Wood Krutch, March, The Twelve Seasons (1949)*

The calendar New Year is the beginning of Winter Solstice so it's a great time to ponder making changes but executing them will more likely occur in the three other life cycles—spring, summer and fall. Spring is the Earth's New Year and our bodies and experiences will have a tendency to match that of nature. Spring comes in gently, gradually and requires patience as we anticipate what is to come. How this cycle might affect you in-the-moment is as follows:

SPRING CYCLE ~ APPROXIMATELY MARCH 20TH TO JUNE 20TH ~ NEW BEGINNINGS AND PLANTING

Cycle Theme: To renew.

Role: To prepare and gently set in motion.

Best at: New thoughts, ideas, growth and introductions.

Challenge(s): Being patient. Balancing transition of being docile to moderately active.

F.I.P.S.S. (FINANCIAL, INTELLECTUAL, PHYSICAL, SOCIAL, SPIRITUAL):

F—Strong time to develop new strategies, thinking and positioning.

I—Strong time to gently execute new ideas and learning from the reflective winter and prior cycles.

P—Strong time to awaken your physical body but not to shock it with too much activity (relative to the physical activity you currently experience).

So—Strong time to begin to re-introduce yourself to people you haven't seen or talked to since the fall cycle.

Sp—Strong time to slowly open yourself up to new practices, or re-introduce yourself to productive old ones.

Spring Observations: Ground hog and other animals begin to emerge, buds on trees and bushes, birds building nests, animals mating, baby animals emerging, indoor plants growing new sprigs, gardens/crops/fields are being prepared for planting and/or being planted, outdoor bugs are beginning to show themselves (in seasonal climates). What do you observe in your climate?

Summer—Execution and Growth...
"Rev your engines!"

"Summer is when we believe, all of a sudden, that if we just walked out the back door and kept on going long enough and far enough we would reach the Rocky Mountains."

—Edward Hoagland, *A Year As It Turns,*
The Tugman's Passage (1982)

It's time to kick it up for summer. You're likely to move forward at a more accelerated pace. Summer is loud, turn on your music in your car, go for a fast paced walk outside. It's a social type of cycle. This season cycle might affect you in-the-moment as follows:

Summer Cycle ~ approximately June twentieth to September twentieth ~ Execution and Growth

Cycle Theme: To move forward.

Role: To assertively and consistently set in motion.

Best at: Bringing thoughts into physical reality.

Challenge(s): Controlling the chaos and speed of the season (can be disorienting).

F.I.P.S.S. (Financial, Intellectual, Physical, Social, Spiritual):

F—Strong time to bring new strategies and ideas into the physical.

I—Strong time to experience life rather than read and reflect.

P—Strong time to actively move your physical body to its peak level.

So—Strong time to be with people regularly and experience high social activity.

Sp—Strong time to consistently and openly practice your rituals and ceremonies.

Summer Observations: Daylight longer, spring flowers (daffodils, tulips) are gone, bright summer flowers emerge and are in full bloom, many of nature's babies are leaving their nests, gardens/crops/fields are being harvested for consumption, indoor plants are flowering, frogs, crickets and other bugs are abundant (in seasonal climates). What do you observe in your climate?

FALL—CELEBRATION AND HARVEST... "TAKING DOWN THE TEMPO."

"For man, autumn is a time of harvest, of gathering together. For nature, it is a time of sowing, of scattering abroad."
—*Edwin Way Teale, Autumn Across America (1956), 14*

The fall can be a very chaotic transition from summer. Even if you didn't take a holiday trip, coming off summer is like coming off of a long vacation. If your schedule is consistent, it still feels very different transitioning into September and the excitement builds for the many upcoming holidays, festivals and school transitions. Fall is a get busy and prepare for, while at the same time, finish up type of cycle. This cycle might affect you in-the-moment as follows:

FALL CYCLE ~ APPROXIMATELY SEPTEMBER 20TH TO DECEMBER 20TH ~ CELEBRATION AND HARVEST

Cycle Theme: Final manifestation(s)/results.

Role: To bring to a close. To prepare for reflection/winter.

Best at: Harvesting and celebrating while easing into a slower reflective/winter tempo.

Challenge(s): Increasing the chaos surrounded by manifestation deadlines as opposed to gently transitioning into next cycle.

F.I.P.S.S. (FINANCIAL, INTELLECTUAL, PHYSICAL, SOCIAL, SPIRITUAL):

F—Strong time to measure success, understand strengths and challenges and make some changes (before winter).

I—Strong time to consider what new learning and meaning winter reflection may bring.

P—Strong time to celebrate strength developed in summer, moving your physical body to a consistent pace to ease into winter.

So—Strong time to balance inner and outer circle interaction.

Sp—Strong time to consistently practice your rituals and ceremonies to create long-term patterns.

Fall Observations: Daylight shorter, bright summer flowers disappear, there seem to be fewer wild animals, garden/crops/fields are prepared for winter rest, indoor plants have less new growth, bees become more aggressive and then they disappear, fewer frogs, crickets and other outdoor bugs (in seasonal climates). What do you observe in your climate?

WINTER—REFLECTION AND HIBERNATION... "ENJOYING THE DOWNTIME."

"Let us love winter, for it is the spring of genius."
—*Pietro Aretino, Letter To Agostino Ricchi, July 10, 1537,"*
TR. Samuel Putnam

My best advice to people who say they hate winter? Learn to love what it symbolizes and what it can truly do for your body, mind and spirit. This is a time to give yourself a break, not to pressure yourself into being overly social or overly active. Read. Veg out! This cycle might affect you in-the-moment as follows:

WINTER CYCLE ~ APPROXIMATELY DECEMBER 20TH TO MARCH 2-^{TH} ~ REFLECTION AND HIBERNATION

Cycle Theme: To reflect. Down time.

Role: To learn. To rest.

Best at: Stillness.

Challenge(s): To accept the winter for the positive it is and not a struggle.

F.I.P.S.S. (FINANCIAL, INTELLECTUAL, PHYSICAL, SOCIAL, SPIRITUAL):

F—Strong time to reflect on success, strengths and accept slow paced challenges.

I—Strong time to learn, listen, read and rest the mind.

P—Strong time to rest physical body, while at the same time move consistently to maintain physical body strength.

So—Strong time to go within and feel less pressured to be available to outer circle.

Sp—Strong time to go within and practice rituals and ceremonies.

Winter Observations: Daylight? (what's that?), quiet nature, stillness, many wild animals are sleeping, people are more sleepy/lethargic, garden/crops/fields are dormant, indoor plants are sustaining, no frogs, crickets and other outdoor bugs (in seasonal climates). What do you observe in your climate?

Personal Years

So we have your Birth Mix—Astrology, Numerology, Birth Order, the cycles of the Earth influences and now Personal Year. This is based on your birth day and month and the current year as a calculation (see "Terms" section). This is similar to the changing seasons but it lasts for a full calendar year. I've provided the cycle vibration along with the Personal Year so you can match the tempo. For instance, if you are having a year with a summer vibration and you are in the summer season, you are likely to kick some major butt in the matched season(s) due simply to the speed in which you are able to manifest. What you have to watch out for is that you don't complete things too fast and miss some important details. Here are some patterns in Personal Years:

- One—New Beginnings and Opportunities (spring/summer vibration)
- Two—Patience and Tact (winter/early spring vibration)
- Three—Social and Light Hearted (summer vibration)
- Four—Harvesting Opportunities (fall vibration)
- Five—Constant Change and Good Fortune (late spring/early summer vibration)
- Six—Balancing Personal Growth and Relationships (late winter/ early spring vibration)
- Seven—Solitude and Rest (winter vibration)
- Eight—Material Rewards (fall vibration)
- Nine—Clutter Clearing (spring vibration)

In this section we'll have a better understanding of how each Personal Year helps us achieve our goals.

PERSONAL YEAR 1—NEW BEGINNINGS AND OPPORTUNITIES… "IN THE BEGINNING…"

"A journey of a thousand miles must begin with a single step."
—**Chinese Proverb**

You have just come off of a year of getting rid of everything that doesn't serve you. You were likely to cut out a bunch of karmic and physical clutter. If you didn't do this, you may spend, at least, the first part of this year making up for lost time. This is a spring/summer vibration so you may find March through September being a major manifestation period for you, so hold onto your hat. However, don't expect to rock your world in six months' time. This is setting the ground work for future butt kicking. It's the little matters that end up adding up to bigger things over time. Some experiences in Year "One" could include:

PERSONAL YEAR 1 ~ NEW BEGINNINGS AND OPPORTUNITIES (SPRING/SUMMER VIBRATION)

Year Theme: To make changes and birth new life ideas that set the tone for the next 9 years!

Role: To take control of your life to manifest your optimal reality.

Best at: Being renewed, new, active, changing.

Challenge(s): Being centered enough to switch gears and make decisions after coming off a purging year.

F.I.P.S.S. (FINANCIAL, INTELLECTUAL, PHYSICAL, SOCIAL, SPIRITUAL):

F—Strong time to change job, career, investment strategies which may require establishing a whole new set of rules.

I—Strong time to consider new learning paths and processes.

P—Strong time to consistently move your physical body and visualize being fit for the rest of your life.

So—Strong time to only keep relationships in your life that move you forward.

Sp—Strong time to decide on your rituals and ceremonies and practice them.

PERSONAL YEAR 2—PATIENCE AND TACT... "DRUM ROLL, PLEASE."

"Do not reveal your thoughts to everyone, lest you drive away your good luck."

—*Apocrypha Ecclesiasticus 8:19*

Year "Two" has a strong energy supporting introverted development. This doesn't mean that you won't be physically fit or successful in all that you set your sights on. It may, however, mean that your approach to all areas of life may be processed a bit more internally and slowly. If anything threatens your inner development it may trigger insecurities. For instance, if an idea isn't fully developed, you may feel like others will try to steal your concept (could be true or perceived). Patience is the key and unveiling at a specific (even calculated) time may be more important to you in this particular year. Some experiences in Year "Two" could be:

PERSONAL YEAR 2 ~ PATIENCE AND TACT (WINTER/EARLY SPRING VIBRATION)

Year Theme: To quietly create.

Role: To be patient, influencing through tact, compromise and cooperation.

Best at: Advancing plans slowly and allowing things to unfold.

Challenge(s): Perceiving situations as struggles rather than opportunities.

F.I.P.S.S. (FINANCIAL, INTELLECTUAL, PHYSICAL, SOCIAL, SPIRITUAL):

F—Strong time to observe and gently and patiently execute money, and career strategies.

I—Strong time to read and research. Less of a pull of energy for travel unless connected with learning/study.

P—Strong time to observe physical set backs as opportunity to stretch (gently) to next level. Energy supports strong intellectual and spiritual development.

So—Strong time to focus on inner circle relationships. Good time for more meaningful interactions.

Sp—Strong time to go within, get quiet, rest within.

PERSONAL YEAR 3—SOCIAL AND LIGHTHEARTED... "PARTY OVER HERE!"

"The best way to prepare for life is to live."
—*Elbert Hubbard, The Note Book (1927)*

Year Three is high energy and fun. It's faster paced than last year. Match this with summer cycle and you're going to feel turbo charged! You've come off of a very reflective year and things that seemed to take forever in your "Two" Year, now seem almost effortless in comparison as long as you can focus. Some experiences in Year "Three" could be:

PERSONAL YEAR 3 ~ SOCIAL AND LIGHT HEARTED (SUMMER VIBRATION)

Year Theme: To creatively expand.

Role: To socialize, create with high energy, and have fun.

Best at: High activity.

Challenge(s): Lacking direction and discipline.

F.I.P.S.S. (FINANCIAL, INTELLECTUAL, PHYSICAL, SOCIAL, SPIRITUAL):

F—Strong time to have fun in your job, career, and enjoy solid finances but must apply some discipline.

I—Strong time to let go and enjoy life experiences. Free flow learning may include additional travel.

P—Strong time for high physical energy which can help keep body fit.

So—Strong time to meet new and exciting people (careful on empty relationships).

Sp—Strong challenge to quiet mind. Creatively combining physical fitness with spiritual approach may be of benefit.

PERSONAL YEAR 4—HARVESTING OPPORTUNITIES… "ONE, TWO, THREE, GO!"

"A wise (wo)man will make more opportunities than s/he finds."
—Francis Bacon, Of Ceremonies And Respects, Essays (1625)

Year "Four" is a year to finalize. The past three years may have felt a bit like a roller coaster. Trail blaze ("One"), go within ("Two"), then back out in the meet new people and experience new ideas ("Three"). But now it's time to reap the rewards. In addition to your expected manifestations, realize that it's likely you unknowingly laid the groundwork for surprise opportunities as well. Some experiences in Year "Four" could be:

PERSONAL YEAR 4 ~ HARVESTING OPPORTUNITIES (FALL VIBRATION)

Year Theme: To reap the harvest (built over the past three years).

Role: To take advantage of any opportunities (planned or surprised).

Best at: Finishing projects.

Challenge(s): Prioritizing the many opportunities so not scattered.

F.I.P.S.S. (FINANCIAL, INTELLECTUAL, PHYSICAL, SOCIAL, SPIRITUAL):

F—Strong time to make sound investments in career, and other financial endeavors.

I—Strong time to be detailed and organized and get into the nuts and bolts of learning.

P—Strong time to revisit physical body issues that haven't been addressed.

So—Strong time to focus on inner circle and functional outer circle.

Sp—Strong time to solidify your rituals and ceremonies and practice them.

PERSONAL YEAR 5—CONSTANT CHANGE AND GOOD FORTUNE... "THINK FAST!"

"Tis better to be fortunate than wise."
— *John Webster, The White Devil (1612), 5.6*

So you've come off a year of opportunities now let's sprinkle on a little luck. The key is to think fast and be flexible. (As my family often says, "Keep a little bend in your knees."). There are times when you won't have a lot of time to make decisions. It's time to trust your intuition so that you receive the full benefits of your "Five" Year. Don't look back and say, "I knew I should've..." Some experiences in Year "Five" could be:

PERSONAL YEAR 5 ~ CONSTANT CHANGE AND GOOD FORTUNE (LATE SPRING/EARLY SUMMER VIBRATION)

Year Theme: To take every advantage of a lucky year.

Role: To optimistically ride the wave of constant opportunities.

Best at: Being quick, raising to next level utilizing intuitive reflexes.

Challenge(s): Being still. Not productive to use old learning for new opportunities.

F.I.P.S.S. (FINANCIAL, INTELLECTUAL, PHYSICAL, SOCIAL, SPIRITUAL):

F—Strong time to change jobs, careers, investment strategies.

I—Strong time to consider new learning paths and processes, particularly through travel.

P—Strong time to consistently move your physical body and be fit for the opportunities that arise.

So—Strong time to keep flexible relationships as you move forward (could also include physically moving).

Sp—Strong time to add flexibility in your rituals and ceremonies, maybe new information.

PERSONAL YEAR 6—BALANCING PERSONAL GROWTH AND RELATIONSHIPS… "LOVE YOU, LOVE ME."

"Growth itself contains the germ of happiness."
—**Pearl S. Buck, To The Young, To My Daughters, With Love (1967)**

You have had two prior years of opportunities, and it's now time to go back inside. Inner circle relationships and personal development will be the prevailing energy for the year. This can be a difficult balance because you may be in demand in regards to your inner circle while you are in contemplation of your direction and growth. Reconsiderations are abundant and this is a staging energy for you to go deeper within yourself next year. Some experiences in Year "Six" could be:

PERSONAL YEAR 6 ~ BALANCING PERSONAL GROWTH AND RELATIONSHIPS (LATE WINTER/EARLY SPRING VIBRATION)

Year Theme: To achieve harmony and balance in all you hold dear.

Role: To be caregiver, comforter and become established in "community" (work, social, non-profit organization…).

Best at: Empathizing. Renewal. Birthing.

Challenge(s): Outer circle social events.

F.I.P.S.S. (FINANCIAL, INTELLECTUAL, PHYSICAL, SOCIAL, SPIRITUAL):

F—Strong time to reconsider or change jobs, careers, investment strategies.

I—Strong time to observe through life experiences, allow intuition to guide.

P—Strong time to consistently move your physical body, being conscious of not overdoing.

So—Strong time to focus on inner circle.

Sp—Strong time to go within to achieve harmony and balance.

PERSONAL YEAR 7—SOLITUDE AND REST… ### "I NEED ALONE TIME."

"The nurse of full-grown souls is solitude."
—*James Russell Lowell, Columbus (1844)*

You began to transition into this last year and now your energy may want to withdraw, to go deep within yourself. This is tough for your inner and outer circle relationships to understand. They may take it personally (you don't care about them, you're being selfish…). It would be a good idea to gently explain your path for the year to maintain your relationships in the future (even if you don't care about them right now). Make no mistake about it, you need this alone time. Don't ignore it. Some experiences in Year "Seven" could be:

PERSONAL YEAR 7 SOLITUDE AND REST (WINTER VIBRATION)

Year Theme: Inner Growth and Reflection.

Role: To focus on you.

Best at: Reading, rest and relaxation.

Challenge(s): Any type of social activity or interaction outside of self.

F.I.P.S.S. (FINANCIAL, INTELLECTUAL, PHYSICAL, SOCIAL, SPIRITUAL):

F—Strong time not to make major changes to jobs, careers, investment strategies.

I—Strong time to study inwardly.

P—Strong time to methodically move your physical body with the added intention of enhancing inward experiences.

So—Strong time to be alone (can be awkward for even social Birth Mixes if not enough alone time).

Sp—Strong time to be on your own and making rituals and ceremonies that fit personal needs.

PERSONAL YEAR 8—MATERIAL REWARDS… "SHOW ME THE MONEY!"

"Money is like a sixth sense without which you cannot make a complete use of the other five."

—*W. Somerset Maugham, Of Human Bondage (1915), 51*

"Eight" is the symbol of infinity and another harvest year. There are two harvest years in the nine year cycle—"Four" and "Eight." It's time to get physical and apply all your managerial skills to get there. All the rest that you experienced last year will be used as fuel for this year. Remember, however, that this is a good year to reap physical benefits but equally a time to experience loss if it is not managed effectively. Don't get too cocky. Some experiences in Year "Eight" could be:

PERSONAL YEAR 8 ~ MATERIAL REWARDS (FALL VIBRATION)

Year Theme: To harvest (of what built over past seven years).

Role: To take advantage of earned opportunities.

Best at: Being efficient, focused and intuitive.

Challenge(s): Allowing for rest.

F.I.P.S.S. (FINANCIAL, INTELLECTUAL, PHYSICAL, SOCIAL, SPIRITUAL):

F—Strong time to receive all material rewards.

I—Strong time to execute your vision and experience physical rewards as opposed to studying or visualizing it.

P— Strong time to focus on keeping your physical body fit.

So—Strong time to focus on your ability to maximize manifesting this year and may not include many inner or outer circle interactions.

Sp—Strong time to independently practice your rituals and ceremonies and make quality time count.

PERSONAL YEAR 9—CLUTTER CLEARING…
"I'M GONNA WASH THAT RIGHT OUT OF MY HAIR."

"Order marches with weighty and measured strides; disorder is always in a hurry."

—*Napoleon I, Maxims (1804-1815)*

So now you're in the last year of this cycle. You've reflected, rebirthed, pursued, and harvested over the past eight years and now it's time to purge physical and spiritual junk that isn't serving you after all your trial and errors. Next year is the beginning of a brand new nine year cycle. Take a deep breath after every purge because there will be many (or, at least, this is what the energy supports). Congratulate yourself after every cosmic confrontation and remind yourself how far you have come. Some experiences in Year "Nine" could be:

PERSONAL YEAR 9 ~ CLUTTER CLEARING (SPRING VIBRATION)

Year Theme: To purge life ideas or items that hold you back in any way.

Role: Soul Clutter buster.

Best at: Preparing, confronting, completion.

Challenge(s): Moving backwards due to fear of letting go.

F.I.P.S.S. (FINANCIAL, INTELLECTUAL, PHYSICAL, SOCIAL, SPIRITUAL):

F—Strong time to purge things in jobs, careers, investment strategies that don't serve higher purpose.

I—Strong time to remove obstacles from new learning paths and processes.

P—Strong time to remove all bad habits connected to your physical body.

So—Strong time to purge relationships that hold you back and adopt positive patterns.

Sp—Strong time to purge old rituals and ceremonies that don't serve your highest good.

V.

Birth Mix and the Balance
of Power—American
Presidents and First Ladies

"The sole advantage of power is that you can do more good."
—Baltasar Gracian, The Art Of Wordly Wisdom (1647), 286, TR,
Joseph Jacobs

W hen researching all Presidents and First Ladies of the United States some interesting trends surfaced:

Astrologically and Numerologically U.S. Presidents trends show (include but not limited to):

- Pisces, Aries or Sagittarians are usually found in the nineteenth century.
- The few Gemini's and Virgos are found in the twentieth century.

- Cancers and Leos were twenty-seven percent of the Presidential mix in the twentieth and twenty-first centuries.
- While Sun Signs are evenly spread, clear trends of "good" and "bad" experiences and number of service years exist in connection with the signs.
- Life Paths "2, 3, 4" and "22/4" are found least.
- Life Paths "1, 3, 22/4" are only found in the nineteenth century.
- The only Life Path "2" is found in the twentieth century (William Henry Harrison didn't count since he died within a month in office).
- Life Path "8" is connected with more Presidents than any other number but only two are in the twentieth century and they inherited the office. Thirty-two (of one-hundred and eleven) years of the nineteenth century or earlier saw Life Path "8's" in office.
- Life Path "6" ranks number one in connection with Presidents' years of service and (with exception to one), all served in the twentieth century and beyond.
- All Life Path "5's" were known for major accomplishments— Thomas Jefferson, Abraham Lincoln, Teddy Roosevelt, and Franklin D. Roosevelt.

Astrologically and Numerologically U.S. First Ladies show (include but not limited to):

- All but one Leo was in office in the twentieth century. The one Leo in the nineteenth century only served as First Lady for one month (her husband died within a month of office) but she was to be the grandmother of another President nearly fifty years later.

- Capricorns and Sagittarians were less likely to become First Ladies and these Astrological Signs were associated with less balanced experiences.
- Gemini's were most active in the nineteenth century and earlier.
- Virgo's were found only in the nineteenth century and earlier and were considered to intensly detailed.
- Life Paths "2, 5, 9" and "22/4" were least prominent.
- Life Path "7" was most prominent with the master number "11/2" coming in second. Most served in the nineteenth century or earlier and combined outnumbered the "7" and "11/2" Presidents.
- Life Path "6" was a more prominent number in the twentieth century (twenty years of the period, 1901-2008).

Overall trends on the balance of divine feminine and masculine (include but not limited to):

- The Presidents and First Ladies (First Ladies Birth Orders that could be found/estimated) were ranked nearly equally on Birth Order:
  #1—Oldest
  #2—Middle
  #3—Only
  #4—Youngest (no First Ladies were recorded as youngest)
- When a President did not have a strong life partner/First Lady, many historians acknowledged that the Presidency was weak as a result (the missing link... balance of the masculine and feminine energies).
- Many First Ladies served as speech writers, attended important meetings in connection with the Presidency or in place of and

served as confidants on major decisions (to what extent we will never really know).

- In the twentieth and twenty-first centuries (combining U.S. Presidents and First Ladies), Life Path "6" influenced over forty percent of the Oval Office terms (1901 thru 2008).

Interestingly enough, the United States official re-birth date is July 4, 1776, and birth mix is Life Path "Five," unending talent; Cancer comforter; "Only," turbo achiever. Like any one-on-one, family or group relationship, this energy or overall group theme has a tendency to support certain Life Paths, Sun Signs and Birth Orders (as demonstrated above). But that's another book.

To break the U.S. Presidents and First Ladies down in detail (date after name is the years in office):

John Adams—1797-1801

birthdate: 10/30/1735—Scorpio, 11/2, Oldest (of three boys)
Abigail Smith Adams
birthdate: 11/11/1744—Scorpio, 11/2, Middle or Oldest girl
(second of four—three girls/one boy)

ADAMS — TWO PRESIDENTS FOR THE PRICE OF ONE:

Abigail, a descendant of many clergy leaders in society, was said to have a great influence over her husband during his Presidency (2nd). She was well-educated and Truman was even quoted as saying "She would be a better president than her husband." She was an advocate of increasing women's rights and talked to the injustice of slavery. Given the complete match on Sun sign and Numerology, it's no surprise the Adams were birds of a feather... methodical Scorpio's, intuitive negotiating "Eleven/Twos." One of John Adams' many notable accomplishments included helping draft the Declaration of Independence (wonder if Abigail wordsmithed?).

John Quincy Adams—1825-29

    birthdate: 7/11/1767—Cancer, 3, Oldest son (second of five)

    Louisa Catherine Johnson Adams

    birthdate: 2/12/1775—Aquarius, 7, Unknown

ADAMS — SASSY MEETS SAVVY:

Louisa was considered very social, political and well traveled. John Q. (6th President) was a man of many words and a fighter and the son of the U.S. 2nd President (John Adams). Louisa brought an Aquarian political, social lightness and savvy along with "Seven" wisdom and vision to the relationship, and the White House. She was credited with getting her husband re-elected (her husband credited with being a stubborn and opinionated "Three"). Lincoln based his Emancipation Proclamation on John Q. Adam's arguments to free slaves.

Chester Alan Arthur—1881-85

    birthdate: 10/5/1829—Libra, 8, Oldest Son (fifth of nine)

    Ellen Lewis Herndon Arthur—Never served

    birthdate: 8/30/1837—Virgo, 3, Only

ARTHURS — THE FORGETTABLES:

While Ellen was known to be very confident, social and accomplished, she passed away before Arthur became the twenty-first President (became President as a result of Garfield's untimely death). Mary Arthur McElroy, his sister, acted as his hostess. This President was known for being fashionable, good looking and some would say added dignity to an office that was not held in very high esteem until then—the Libra preference for beauty and good looks and the "Eight" value of dignity and fashion helped complete that image. But without a true confidant, his time in office was truly forgettable.

James Buchanan—1857-61

> birthdate: 4/23/1791—Taurus, 9, Oldest Son (second of eleven)
>
> Harriet Lane
>
> birthdate: 5/9/1830—Taurus, 8, Only

BUCHANANS — SOCIAL AND CAUTIOUS TAURUS TEAM:

Harriet was this 15th President's niece as Arthur was the only bachelor President. Her parents died and her Uncle became her legal guardian and they became very close. She was a very popular Taurus, was polished, had many admirers (an Only child and "8" dream) and Queen Victoria even approved of her. Her Uncle relied heavily on her as a confidant and hostess. Buchanan was cautious and sat in the middle on issues of slavery (but as a "9" Humanitarian, this path usually supports a greater good to help others). Playing it Taurus safe led to his demise when it came to Presidential accomplishments. He was happy to leave office (similar to Taft). Three other "Nine" Presidents that would hold office are Jimmy Carter (his wife Rosalyn was also a "Nine"), Rutherford Hayes and William Howard Taft.

George H. W. Bush (Sr.)—1989-1993

> birthdate: 6/12/1924—Gemini, 7, Middle (two years between older brother)
>
> Barbara Pierce Bush
>
> birthdate: 6/8/1925—Gemini, 22/4, unknown (third child)

BUSHES — CHARMING GEMINI MASTER NUMBER TEAM:

Barbara (great, great, great uncle is Franklin Pierce—U.S. President 1853-1857 and grandfather was Ohio Supreme Court Justice) was known for her stance on literacy and established a foundation for family literacy. Her "Twenty-two" wisdom could embrace the bigger picture as she held back her opinions to avoid controversy. She chose a similar route to another "Twenty-two/Four" First Lady Mamie Eisenhower. America loved her for her Gemini good-humor and natural demeanor. A war-time President (41ˢᵗ), George H.W. became very popular but the poor economy, large deficit, social progam cut-backs and breaking his promise not to increase taxes ("Read my lips, no new taxes") pushed him out of office. While it wasn't as obvious to the public eye, these two Gemini's along with master number Life Paths would have likely discussed issues on a larger scale similar to John Adams (2ⁿᵈ President), and the Carters.

George W. Bush—2001-2008

birthdate: 7/6/1946—Cancer, 6, Oldest
Laura Welch Bush
birthdate: 11/4/1946—Scorpio, 8, Only

BUSHES — FOLLOWING IN THE FOOTSTEPS:

Laura (degreed in education and a teacher and librarian by profession) took a patient and calculating Scorpio approach and picked up where her mother-in-law left off and focused on literacy and children. Her "Eight" leadership could be viewed as a national extension to her chosen profession. George W. followed in his father's footsteps and became a war-time President (43rd) following the Nine/Eleven Terrorist attack in New York City. While interest rates reached all time lows during his first four years, the economy was experiencing difficult times as war raged on. Upon publishing *Birth Mix Patterns*, it was no surprise that Bush was re-elected to the Oval Office as Americans have had the tendency to support Cancers (U.S. is a Cancer) and Life Path "Sixes" in the twentieth century and beyond. (His 2004 opponent was a "22/4" which has been historically unsuccessful in the Oval Office.)

Jimmy Carter—1977-81

birthdate: 10/1/1924—Libra, 9, Oldest (of four)

Rosalynn Smith Carter

birthdate: 8/18/1927—Leo, 9, Oldest (of four)

CARTERS —THE HUMANITARIANS:

Both Oldest children, the Carters were partners from the peanut farm business to the Presidency (39th) and then, ultimately the 2002 Nobel Peace Prize (very "9" fulfilling). Rosalyn was known to attend Cabinet meetings and important briefings (similar to the Tafts). Jimmy Carter (just by his first name) reveals his down to Earth approach and preferred to be seen as the "people's President." Like the Adams' (2nd President) partnership, their similar Life Path numbers strongly led the Carters in a "Nine" direction. The Libra may have kept the President sitting too long on certain issues until perfect harmony was achieved. The Leo and Oldest child in Rosalyn enhanced her generosity and her ability to help her husband lead and make decisions. For the most part, "9's" seem to be less content in the Oval Office.

Grover Cleveland—1885-89 & 1893-97

birthdate: 3/18/1837—Pisces, 4, Middle (two years between older brother, fifth of nine)

Frances Folsom Cleveland

birthdate: 7/21/1864—Cancer, 11/2, Only

CLEVELANDS — "GRACE" AND GROVER:

Frances loved being in the White House and was not political but very social (more of a "Two" peacemaker, Cancer lover not a fighter). She was said to be beautiful, was 27 years his junior, and her style (clothing, hair...) was imitated by many women at that time, and surely as a Cancer, loved to be loved. A Pisces can have an impractical style and Grover (22nd President) ran wild as a young man and fathered an illegitimate child. He settled down, worked ("Four") hard, became known for being blunt and courageous ("Four" stubbornly) battling corruption. When they left the White House the first time, Frances (with her "Eleven" intuitive vision and "Only" goal-orientation) announced that they would be back another term and they did just that four years later.

William J. Clinton—1993-2001

> birthdate: 8/19/1946—Leo, 11/2, Only (younger half brother,
> 8 year difference)
> Hillary Rodham Clinton
> birthdate: 10/26/1947—Scorpio, 3, Oldest

CLINTONS — UNLADYLIKE AND OVERLYMANLIKE:

Hillary was a lawyer by trade and was appointed head of the task force for health care reform. Her (very "3," but traditionally unFirst Ladylike) leadership role was unpopular so she took her activism down a notch. The patient Scorpio, once her husband left the White House, ran and was elected for U.S. Senate (first time a First Lady has been elected to public office). While "Bill" Clinton oversaw a country with a healthy economy for eight years, this (42nd) President's Leo charm overtook his "Eleven" vision and couldn't shake the justified accusations of sexual misconduct which led to an impeachment trial. In addition there were multiple investigations on questionable business dealings in his home state. With Scorpio commitment and longer range goals in mind, Hillary stood by her man the entire time.

Calvin Coolidge—1923-29

birthdate: 7/4/1872—Cancer, 2, Oldest (of two)

Grace Anna Goodhue Coolidge

birthdate: 1/3/1879—Capricorn, 11/2, Only

COOLIDGES — GIVE TO GET:

Grace was known for her elegance. A Capricorn and Only child state-ment through and through, she was quoted, "This was I and yet not I" as she followed her husband's path (a Capricorn unable to climb... an Only unable to reach her personal goals). President Coolidge (30th) was a man of few words and some believe that the reason why Coolidge (more of a Peacemaker and less of a visionary) was re-elected was because of his wife's outstanding "Eleven" vision and abilities to make everyone feel comfortable (his 6 years included taking over after Harding's death then ran for re-election).

Dwight Eisenhower—1953–61

birthdate: 10/14/1890—Libra, 6, Middle (third of seven sons)

Mamie Geneva Doud Eisenhower

birthdate: 11/14/1896—Scorpio, 22/4, Middle (second of four girls)

EISENHOWERS — HOME IS WHERE THE HEART IS:

Dwight Eisenhower (34th President) was a five-star General before he took office. Before his Presidency this Libra rebalanced/restructured the U.S. war department, (process-oriented "Six") assisted in the creation of NATO, and as President oversaw the most prosperous U.S. economy since the 1920's. Interestingly enough, like some other "Sixes" in this of-fice, Eisenhower suffered a physical setback, a heart attack (it was mild). The life partner that could have kept up with him would be multi-faceted Life Path "Twenty-two" and persevering Scorpio, Mamie. Her choice was to support "Ike" to enable him to save the world (as a war hero and beyond). She smoothed out his rough edges, was an accomplished hostess, and made a comfortable home wherever they pitched tent. She won the hearts of the public with her warm, confident feminine style while still running the White House with efficiency and authority. She stayed out of politics making her career "Ike" which, in essence, catapulted him to success.

Millard Fillmore—1850–53

birthdate: 1/7/1800—Capricorn, 8, Oldest son (second of nine)

Abigail Powers Fillmore

birthdate: 3/13/1798—Pisces, 5, Oldest girl (of two/other was boy)

FILLMORES — SELF-MADE TEAM:

Millard (13th President) inherited the office when Zachary Taylor died and was known for being "Eight" level-headed and confident but lacked a clear platform on abolishing slavery (which Taylor was willing to fight for). Millard (Capricorn climber) met Abigail in school (both of hardworking, self-made roots). His wife was an avid reader (as he was) and whenever Millard traveled he would always bring books back for the family library. Being allowed to believe in her (Pisces) dreams, she was the first First Lady to continue working after marriage. She loved to learn and teach (an unending talent "Five" that couldn't devour information fast enough to satisfy her appetite). When she did stop working, after her first daughter was born, she created the first library in the White House, studied French and piano and never stopped reading. Believing in her husband's dreams (Pisces), she even attended political debates to advise her husband. Once Millard left office, he finished his career as the president of a historical society.

Gerald Ford—1974–77

(parents' marriage: Only/father's and mother's second marriages
had three more siblings each)

birthdate: 7/14/1913—Cancer, 8, Only

Elizabeth Bloomer Ford

birthdate: 4/8/1918—Aries, 4, Oldest/Only daughter (third child)

FORDS — OPEN CHALLENGES, OPEN INSPIRATION:

Gerald Ford was a football star sought by a number of professional teams (skipped the money that "Eights" can be very fond of), but went into politics, eventually inheriting the office (38th President) after Nixon's resignation. Ford showed his supporter/comforter side (Cancer) when he pardoned Nixon of any crimes committed during his Presidency but this didn't win him votes for the next Presidency. "Betty" had many life challenges that took "Four" hard work to get past including a divorce in her 20's (before meeting Ford), breast cancer, alcoholism and drug addiction. A result of her "roll up her sleeves" hard "Four" work, she created the Betty Ford Center helping others overcome drug and alcohol dependency. She led by Aries inspiration and was a supporter of the Equal Rights Amendment for women even though openly opposed by her husband. By the end of her husband's term, she was admired to the point of campaign buttons saying "Keep Betty in the White House."

James Garfield—1881

birthdate: 11/19/1831—Scorpio, 7, Only (youngest of five; five years
between him and older brother)

Lucretia Rudolph Garfield—Did not serve

birthdate: 4/19/1832—Aries, 1, Oldest (of four)

GARFIELDS — SHORT-LIVED (LITERALLY):

The Garfield's didn't get a chance to influence the nation via the White

House as James was shot (assassinated) and died two months after entering the Oval Office. The forgettable Arthur would take his place.

Ulysses S. Grant—1869-77
   birthdate: 4/27/1822—Taurus, 8, Oldest (of six)
   Julia Dent Grant
   birthdate: 1/26/1826—Aquarius, 8, Oldest

GRANTS — "8" IT UP:

Ulysses was a general and national military hero and was voted in as (the 18th) President. Julia was living her dream to be able to have grand events (fun-loving Aquarius) and spend lots of money ("Eight" fantasy). Ulysses being an "Eight" himself focused on money matters as well and how to restore economic order but was unable to do much more as corruption (history tells it), unbeknownst to him, became widespread among those thought to be friends (sometimes Taurus are just too trusting) of the President. But the Grants had a (Taurus/Aquarius) comfortable and loving family life, and were loved by all and treated well even following the scandals. In death, our "Eight" couple are buried in an elaborate tomb in New York City.

Warren Harding—1921-23
   birthdate: 11/2/1865—Scorpio, 6, Oldest (of eight)
   Florence Kling Harding
   birthdate: 8/15/1860—Leo, 2, Unknown

HARDINGS — SCANDALOUS MIX:

Warren Harding was not inclined to be President but his wife, nicknamed "the Duchess" (coming from a wealthy family), had other plans. She was ready to Leo shine and he became the (29th) President with her strong encouragement (and her knowing that it could be to his demise... as told to her by a psychic). However, history would seem to support that Warren Harding's mix of Scorpio patience with "Six" creative, heart-centered abilities were the makings of an effective President. But scandal after scandal revolved around friends getting paid for developing federally-owned oil fields (Teapot Dome Affair), the attorney general was tried for corruption, alcohol was served in the White House to his friends during prohibition and more. While he wasn't directly connected to any of the scandals, and was intending on going on a speaking tour to reduce the negative press, he died in office before this could happen. Some say he died from a heart attack, others an embolism, others say it began with food poisoning. But upon his death Florence burned most of the deceased President's papers at the White House and she died 15 months later.

Benjamin Harrison—1889-93

 birthdate: 8/20/1833—Leo, 7, Middle (fifth of thirteen; second
  in ten in second marriage)
 Caroline Lavinia Scott Harrison
 birthdate: 10/1/1832—Libra, 7, Middle (second girl of three plus
  two boys)

HARRISONS — SUPER "7'S":

Caroline was educated at Farmer's College (where her father taught), was a major supporter of women's rights, the president and organizer of Daughters of the American Revolution and helped John Hopkins raise funds for his medical school on the condition that he would admit women. She updated the White House adding electricity, indoor bathrooms, a modernized kitchen and overhauled the interior. She was able to achieve true Libra balance by championing women's programs and bringing the feminine energy into more of a balance in the country overall. Being an expert

"Seven" she, personally, was a scholar and looked to expand women's education to enable them to achieve the same. She and her husband were a great "Seven" match as she balanced out Benjamin's tendency to take on a bit of the "Seven" colder traits (and being detailed to a fault). This (23rd) President's grandfather was the ninth President (William Henry Harrison) and his father was a Congressman. He was an accomplished leader in the military, and said to be a brilliant lawyer. As a Leo President Benjamin Harrison shined, six states were admitted to the Union, he shaped foreign policy, and signed the Sherman Anti-trust Act to limit unfair monopolies and unfair trade. On his Presidential journey, a one-billion dollar peace time budget was highly criticized and the Sherman Silver Bill in 1890 would trigger (three years later) the 1893 Panic/Stock Market Crash. A very accomplished team with a laundry list of accomplishments (with some accomplishments come some failures).

William Henry Harrison—1841

> birthdate: 2/9/1773—Aquarius, 2, Oldest son (youngest of seven)
> Anna Tuthill Symmes Harrison
> birthdate: 7/25/1775—Leo, 7, Only (raised by Grandparents)

HARRISONS — WISE GRANDMOTHER HARRISON:

William Henry's father was one of signers of the Declaration of Independence and George Washington was a friend of the family. He was an accomplished military man with much of his fighting to do with Native American Indians. He was the oldest man elected to the White House (9th) and died within one month of being sworn into office (first President to die in office). Anna (a master number and leader Leo) was the first President's wife to receive a formal education and grandmother to the 23rd President.

Rutherford B. Hayes—1877-81

> birthdate: 10/4/1822—Libra, 9, Youngest (of five/sickly child—seven years between him and older brother, two sisters in between them)
>
> Lucy Ware Hayes
>
> birthdate: 8/28/1831—Virgo, 4, Oldest Girl (two older brothers)

HAYES — BALANCE AND HEAL:

Lucy is the first First Lady to earn a college degree. She is best remembered for banning alcohol in the White House. Rutherford (19ᵗʰ President) was known for his high moral standards. Both he and his wife focused heavily on the reform of mental hospitals showing his "Nine" compassion and Lucy also expanded to increasing care for indigent women without outwardly supporting the women's rights movement revealing her "Four" ability to problem solve but in a less controversial way to compliment her life partner's needs. Rutherford was known for restoring dignity to the office of President that was so full of scandal with Grant's administration. Who better to do this than the Virgo healer and Libra balancer who looks to his/her environment and work to be a direct reflection of him/her.

Herbert Hoover—1929-33

> birthdate: 8/10/1874—Leo, 11/2, Middle (second son of three, three years between him and older brother)
>
> Lou Henry Hoover
>
> birthdate: 3/29/1874—Aries, 7, Oldest (of two girls)

HOOVERS — GENEROSITY AND (MASTER NUMBER) VISION:

Lou Henry was the first woman to earn a Geology degree at Stanford University. She encouraged (with her Aries inspiration) women to be physically active, be active in their communities and volunteer to help the less fortunate and did this (most prevalently) through the Girl Scouts. When entertaining and redecorating many areas in the White House, the Hayes (Lou's "Seven" unshakeable focus and Herbert's "Eleven" vision and Leo generosity) used their own money to further emphasize the need for the country to be charitable and thrifty. Herbert (31st President) was an Engineer ("Eleven" intellectual) by training and could be seen as coldly scientific. The Hoover Presidency was negatively marked by the Stock Market Crash of 1929 and Herbert was largely blamed for the Great Depression but Lou would be known as being one of the most charitable First Ladies in history.

Andrew Jackson—1829-37

> birthdate: 3/15/1767—Pisces, 3, Youngest (of three sons; two years difference above him)
>
> Rachel Donelson Robards Jackson—Never served birthdate: 6/15/1767—Gemini, 6, Middle (four of twelve)

JACKSONS — DRAMA AND DISAGREEMENTS:

Rachel, a strong frontier woman would die from a heart attack ("Six" taking things to heart) before her husband took office due to the stress of slander against her while her husband was campaigning for the Presidency. (Rachel's niece would become hostess for the 7th President.) Andrew was the first "poor boy" to become President and was known to represent the "common man." By the time he was fourteen his youngest child dependence would grow into independence as both his parent's and siblings all died by the time he was fourteen. The "Three" Jackson's fiery statements and dramatic Pisces body language are recorded throughout history and he signed so many vetoes that he outnumbered vetoes of the first six presidents put together. No family, no life partner confidant, no talkin' to him.

Thomas Jefferson—1801-09

> birthdate: 4/13/1743—Aries, 5, Oldest son (third of ten)
>
> Martha Wayles Skelton Jefferson—Never served
>
> birthdate: 10/19/1748—Libra, 4, Oldest (had younger sister)

JEFFERSONS — EVER EXPANDING:

Martha was dead nearly 20 years by the time Jefferson (3rd President) was in the White House so he was less formal and called on Dolley Madison (wife of Secretary of State) to be hostess if needed. He was known and respected as an inspirational leader (common among Aries) supporting individual rights, religious freedom as well as freedom of speech, being the creator of the words "All men are created equal" and "All men are entitled to life, liberty and the pursuit of happiness" within the Declaration of Independence. As a Life Path "Five" unending talent, he was a map maker instead of an observer. He viewed being the founder (or father) of the University of Virginia as being the higher accomplishment in his life rather than being the President of the United States for eight years.

Andrew Johnson—1865-69

> birthdate: 12/29/1808—Capricorn, 22/4, Youngest (of three,
>
>   second son, four years between him and older brother)
>
> Eliza McArdle Johnson
>
> birthdate: 10/4/1810—Libra, 6, Only

JOHNSONS — CLIMBING FROM HUMBLE BEGINNINGS:

While Eliza was an invalid due to tuberculosis, she was a very supportive Life Path "Six" (to the 17th President) while in the White House (particularly during his impeachment trial) and his Libra balance. Andrew Johnson always acknowledged his partnership with his wife as he succeeded in business and then politics (she was well educated for her time even with a poor background). Both Andrew and Eliza had humble beginnings. He had a strong belief in keeping government out of people's business. A Life Path "Twenty-two/Four" (material and spiritual master) and Capricorn (climber), he climbed out of the poverty and into the highest ranking office in the land. His Presidency ended while still in office as the political community dismissed and disgraced him through impeachment (acquitted but put on trial) as a result of conflicting views and actions with his party and Congress.

Lyndon Johnson—1963-69

birthdate: 8/27/1908—Virgo, 8, Oldest (of five)

Claudia Taylor Johnson

birthdate: 12/12/1912—Sagittarius, 1, Oldest girl (two older brothers)

JOHNSONS — BEAUTY AND THE (CYNICAL) BEAST:

Claudia was called "ladybird" as a result of her beauty. She was said to be very clever (degreed in Journalism) and kept her composure in the toughest of situations (showing her "One" leadership in a less aggressive way) interacting with her intense "Eight" husband, at times, bossiness and criticism in public. She was supportive but also believed in doing "whatever makes your heart sing" (classic Sag). This (36th) President was known for his ambition and took his oath when JFK was assassinated. With the Vietnam war, death of many people and riots flaring, the Virgo healer in him sought peace by not seeking re-election (helping the "Eight" in him find his spirit).

John F. Kennedy—1961-63

> birthdate: 5/29/1917—Gemini, 7, Middle (second of nine, two years between him and older brother)
>
> Jacqueline Bouvier Kennedy
>
> birthdate: 7/28/1929—Leo, 11/2, Oldest daughter

KENNEDYS — CLEVER, CHIC AND CHARMING:

JFK (35th President) and Jacqueline were both master numbers and left their marks as individuals. Jacqueline was a symbol of Leo chic. Born in a world of privilege, she had all the training and makings of a U.S. twentieth century dignitary. Her "Eleven" vision of the role of the First Lady put the entire world in awe. JFK, known for his "Eleven" thinker approach and Gemini charm, was the youngest President elected to office. He had great impact before his life was taken only two years into his Presidency and America loved him. His many accomplishments included human rights legislation, tax reform, controls on nuclear arms, and acceleration of the space program.

Abraham Lincoln—1861-65

> birthdate: 2/12/1809—Aquarius, 5, Oldest son (of three)
>
> Mary Todd Lincoln
>
> birthdate: 12/13/1818—Sagittarius, 7, Middle (of sixteen—7 first family/9 second family)

LINCOLNS — VISION ENDING IN TRAGEDY:

Abraham Lincoln, like Thomas Jefferson, was a Life Path "Five." He was a man of discipline: self-schooled, practiced law and ultimately became the (16th) U.S. President who changed the course of history with his Emancipation Proclamation making slavery illegal. Mary was said to be intelligent and witty when Abraham Lincoln met her—a "Seven" intellectual that had an interest in politics and the drive to see him succeed—but it was a difficult time when the Lincolns were in the White House. Threatening mail from U.S. citizens, her not fitting into Washington society (a Sag nightmare as they thrive on being the life of the party), the war and the death of her second son while in the White House was unbearable. When Abe Lincoln was assassinated and then her youngest son died at 18 she was mentally unreachable.

James Madison—1809-1817

birthdate: 3/16/1751—Pisces, 6, Oldest (of twelve)

Dorothea Payne Todd Madison aka Dolley Madison

birthdate: 5/20/1768—Taurus (cusp Gemini), 11/2, Oldest (of four girls)

MADISONS — SOCIAL, CHARMING AND ACCOMPLISHED VISION:
Dolley Madison was hostess for the White House not only for her husband's 6 years in office but also Thomas Jefferson (since his wife had passed). Dolley was known to be quite the entertainer while being Taurus balanced and unpretentious at the same time. When being forced from the White House when the British invaded and burnt it to the ground, her "Eleven" vision resulted in saving many treasures including the Declaration of Independence and George Washington's portrait. James Madison, the 4th U.S. President and a "Six" organizer that strived to develop tools to help others and the Pisces believing in his and others' dreams of equality (continuing Jefferson's work), was known as "The Father of the Constitution."

William McKinley—1897-1901

> birthdate: 1/29/1843—Aquarius, 1, Only or Middle (seventh of
> nine; five plus years between him and older brother)
> Ida Saxton McKinley
> birthdate: 6/8/1847—Gemini, 7, Middle (second of three)

McKINLEYS — INNOVATORS WITH TARGETED FOCUS:

While Ida had seizures and difficulty walking she (the fun-loving Gemini overcoming a potential "Seven" isolation pattern) would still attend functions, and if she went into seizure William would simply put a handkerchief over her face and remove it as if nothing happened. William (25th President) was known for his ("One" leadership and Aquarius ability to manifest original ideas) ability to create a prosperous America and won his second term on the campaign "Four years more of the full dinner pail" only to meet with an assassin's bullet before serving his next term. Then, in walks ready and able Teddy Roosevelt.

James Monroe—1817-25

> birthdate: 4/28/1758—Taurus, 8, Oldest (of five)
> Elizabeth Kortwright Monroe
> birthdate: 6/30/1768—Cancer, 4, Middle (of six)

MONROES — GOING "8" ALONE:

While Cancer's are known for their nurturing traits, Elizabeth was cold and aloof. She was said to be very beautiful, but had epilepsy and in those days people treated this like a mental health issue which pushed her further away from Washington society (the opposite of how Ida McKinley handled her seizures). Many "Fours" have to work hard to reach their goals and she was able to move with grace into overcoming her illness becoming "la belle Americaine" in France. It's no wonder she even redecorated the President's House (not called the White House at that time) with French rather than American furniture which became very controversial. She played little role in James Monroe's (5ᵗʰ) Presidency or political career. The Monroe Document would be his most widely known accomplishment as it declared the American continent off limits to European colonization (an "Eight" move to help America prosper as the United States). But as "Eights" sometimes do, he didn't manage his personal money affairs and lost his Virginia plantation (a major blow to the spirit of a Taurus who looks for the security of hearth and home).

Richard Nixon—1969-74

birthdate: 1/9/1913—Capricorn, 6, Middle (second of five sons; four years difference between him and older brother)

Thelma "Pat" Catherine Ryan Nixon

birthdate: 3/16/1912—Pisces, 5, Oldest girl (two older brothers)

NIXONS — PISCES PERCEPTIONS AND PROTECTION:

Pat was dedicated to Richard's (37ᵗʰ President) political success but hated the slander and eventually asked him to leave politics (the perceptive Pisces). But his "Six" need to serve others and Capricorn drive finally led him to the office of President. While she had the dynamic Life Path "Five" of Jefferson and Lincoln, she distanced herself from the media and other events to protect herself (smart for a Pisces). This resulted in the media labeling her "Plastic Pat." Her Pisces intuition had served her well as this distance helped get her and her husband through his impeachment (Watergate).

Franklin Pierce—1853-57

birthdate: 11/23/1804—Sagittarius, 11/2, Middle (seventh of eight
for father, sixth of eight second marriage, one year between him
and older brother)

Jane Means Appleton Pierce

birthdate: 3/12/1806—Pisces, 3, Unknown

PIERCES — A SOUL-LESS LEADERSHIP:

Jane could have been an outspoken person, similar to John Q. Adams or
Hillary Clinton but instead she became "a shadow in the White House."
This was her way of communicating her disapproval of her husband being
in politics. Her dreams continued to be snuffed out and crushed her Pisces soul as she lost all three of her sons while her husband held political
offices. Her lack of dedication, some say, resulted in her husband's ineffec-
tive stint as the 14th President. While Franklin was known to be a good
looking, cheerful Sagittarian and one that persevered in the face of adversity (an accomplished soldier), he faced many challenges that couldn't be
overcome — family tragedies and political career (attempting to acquire
Cuba, sponsored legislation that ended in major bloodshed on the slavery
issues...) that eventually lost his nomination for re-election.

James Polk—1845-49

birthdate: 11/2/1795—Scorpio, 8, Oldest (of ten)

Sarah Childress Polk

birthdate: 9/4/1803—Virgo, 7, Middle (third of six)

POLKS — INTENSELY DETAILED:

Sarah was a well-educated, well-informed woman and a Virgo focusing
on serving the greater good from her perspective as she banned drinking, dancing and card playing (more work and less play made her Scorpio, "Eight" husband even more intense than he already was) in the White

House and preferred men's political discussions to women's small talk. James Polk (11ᵗʰ President) married Sarah to help advance his political career. She, a "Seven" intellectual, immediately became his private secretary. They both worked long hours when James became President. Sarah's Virgo detail and "Seven" vision had a major influence on his politics. In fact, he trusted no other person with details (even his own cabinet). He literally worked himself to death being too detailed and controlling and died the same year he left office but left with successfully stimulating free trade and revived a policy that would establish the nation's financial system. Very "Eight"ly.

Ronald Reagan—1981-89

> birthdate: 2/6/1911—Aquarius, 11/2, Youngest (of two sons; two
>   year difference)
> Nancy Davis Reagan
> birthdate: 7/6/1921—Cancer, 8, Only

REAGANS — LOVED, LOVING AND LOVEABLE:

Ronald Reagan (40ᵗʰ President) was loved by many (with his Aquarian and Youngest born charm) and his administration was known for creating a more prosperous America and strengthening the idea of world peace. His "Two/Eleven" negotiation talents proved extremely valuable, particularly with the Soviet Union when intermediate-range nuclear missiles were eliminated. It's no surprise that Nancy Reagan is a Cancer as she was very dedicated to her husband, complimented with "Eight" majestic leadership (with some "Eight" whoopsies like having lavish inaugural celebrations and spending a large amount of money redecorating the private quarters of the White House) and reputation for being commanding (some called her the "Assistant President"). Her strength as First Lady was demonstrated internationally as she pulled in First Ladies from 17 different countries to strategize on how to fight alcohol and drug abuse among young people worldwide. A great compliment for the White House.

Franklin D. Roosevelt—1933-45

> birthdate: 1/30/1882—Aquarius, 5, Only
>
> Anna Eleanor Roosevelt
>
> birthdate: 10/11/1884—Libra, 6, Oldest daughter

ROOSEVELTS — INNOVATIVE SERVICE:

Both Franklin and Eleanor have gone down in history as two very accomplished and respected individuals. Franklin, the only U.S. President (32nd) elected for three terms, was an out-of-the-box "Aquarian" thinker. Revamping the U.S. systems and his "Five" creative programs got the economy back on its feet (but not without much controversy). Eleanor was known as the First Lady of the World with her Libra ability of manifesting beauty and balance and "Six" drive to serve others (including her husband when he was stricken with Polio). As First Lady she wrote 70 speeches, 2,500 newspaper columns, and 300 magazine articles on her many causes including the advancement of women, the poor/disadvantaged and civil rights for African Americans. After her husband's death she was appointed to the United Nations and was instrumental in drafting the Declaration of Human Rights.

Theodore Roosevelt—1901-09

> birthdate: 10/27/1858—Scorpio, 5, Oldest son (second of four)
>
> Edith Kermit Carow Roosevelt
>
> birthdate: 8/6/1861—Leo, 3, Unknown

ROOSEVELTS — LAND, LADIES AND LAW ENFORCEMENT:

Teddy "spoke softly but carried a big stick." This Scorpio statement demonstrated the patience of waiting until it was the right time to strike (then striking hard). Both Teddy (26th President) and Franklin D. were unending talent "Five's." Teddy demonstrated this by being the youngest President in office of his time, allocating 150 million acres to increase America's forest reserve, and aiming efforts at decreasing business corruption (no doubt an extension of his passion in law enforcement). While Teddy was pounding his fist on podiums, Edith, with Leo grace and concern for her circle of cubs, contracted building an extension on the White House, allowing them to expand the private living quarters for their five children. As a "Three" communicator her expression was more through her actions as a visionary. Armed with the knowledge that the Presidents have only been as effective as their life partners, she officially began the First Ladies portrait gallery.

William H. Taft—1909-13

birthdate: 9/15/1857—Virgo, 9, Middle (seventh of ten; second of five in second marriage, two years between him and older brother)

Helen Herron Taft

birthdate: 6/2/1861—Gemini, 6, Middle (4th of eleven)

TAFTS — SUPREME VERSUS SOCIAL:

Helen had the drive to be in the White House (as First Lady) and the only way to do this would be for her husband to become President (26th). When he won, Helen was the first wife to ride in the inaugural carriage. She sat in most of Taft's meetings and would discuss her opinions with him in private (a "Six" organizer and creator). Helen, Gemini, loved traveling, embraced change and the excitement and pace that revolved around events within the White House. Taft was a "Nine" Humanitarian and really wanted to be a Supreme Court Justice which would allow him to express his detailed Virgoness and serve the greater good. While Helen was devastated when her husband lost for re-election, he was glad to go and later was appointed to a Supreme Court seat.

Zachary Taylor—1849-50

birthdate: 11/24/1784—Sagittarius, 1, Middle (third of nine; third son; boy two years above him)

Margaret Mackall Smith Taylor

birthdate: 9/21/1788—Virgo, 9, Unknown

TAYLORS — A WAR HERO'S DEMISE OFF THE FIELD:

Zachary Taylor was a war hero that knew nothing about politics but was elected on his war service merits. While "Ones" have made great leaders in many areas, the Presidency (12th) has not usually been a productive place for this Life Path number. He led a very hot debate in relation to Southern Succession and threatened to lead the army himself to hang anyone against the Union. However, he died in office after only 15 months and this fight was over until Lincoln took office. Margaret, with a smile on her face, followed her husband from post to post during his war-time service utilizing her Virgo organizational talents and "9"ability to see the need for compassion and humanity in each war-time situation. But when it came to the Presidency, she chose not to participate and her daughter hosted receptions (partially due to her health) and (oddly enough) was very concerned about what this would do to her husband's health.

Harry Truman—1945-53

birthdate: 5/8/1884—Taurus, 7, Oldest (of three)

Elizabeth Virginia Wallace Truman

birthdate: 2/13/1885—Aquarius, 1, Oldest

TRUMANS — REBUILDERS:

While Elizabeth put on a public show of being a demure woman, she was said, in private, to be Harry Truman's closest confident, advisor, and even speech writer (a true "One" expression with creative Aquarius flair). He said he discussed all important decisions with her and "her judgment was always good." Truman took office (33rd President) when FDR passed on and was completely unprepared for the job that was held by his predecessor for nearly twelve years. He made very difficult decisions like dropping the atom bomb on Hiroshima and Nagasaki (goes against the grain of a Taurus), worked diligently on the post WWII reconstruction and the U.N. (very Taurus-like), introduced the Truman Doctrine with the vision of containing communism which brought on the Cold War and that was just his first term. He was known as being very determined ("Seven" focus and Taurus stubborn) but had enough and didn't seek re-election.

John Tyler—1841-45

> birthdate: 3/29/1790—Aries, 22/4, Middle (sixth of eight; second son; boy two years above him)
>
> Letitia Christian Tyler
>
> birthdate: 11/12/1790—Scorpio, 4, Middle (seventh of twelve)
>
> Julia Gardner Tyler
>
> birthdate: 5/4/1820—Taurus, 2, Oldest Girl (two brothers, one younger sister)

TYLERS — TOO MUCH, TOO LITTLE, TOO LATE:

Letitia, Tyler's first wife, was sickly, uneducated and trained to be a "good southern wife." By 1842 she died of a stroke. He then met and married Julia, thirty years younger than John, in 1844. She was ready for Washington society but only had eight months to socialize. She had a number of parties to make her (Taurus friendly) mark and managed to make her unpopular husband (10ᵗʰ President) appear successful as she promoted ("Two" socially negotiated) some of his programs while entertaining. John Tyler was the first Vice President to be elevated to President but congress and the cabinet called him "His Accidency." His politics were not as Whig-like as his predecessor, and he dug his heals in pretty quickly (being more stubborn "Four" than balanced "Twenty-two"), nearly all of his cabinet quit, and the House of Representatives tried to impeach him for wrongful use of veto power (it didn't hold up but the conflict was clear). His ability to lead by Aries inspiration was, obviously, not achieved.

Martin Van Buren—1837-41

birthdate: 12/5/1782—Sagittarius, 8, Middle (third of five)
Hannah Hoes Van Buren
birthdate: 3/8/1783—Pisces, 3, Unknown

VAN BURENS — SUAVE BUT LACKED COMMITMENT:
Hannah crossed over before Martin took office (as 8ᵗʰ President) so his daughter-in-law served as hostess. Martin had no life partner to share the office with. He was known for being non-committal. He was a smooth Sag talker but spent too much time weighing all the options. The financial panic in 1837 closing 618 banks was what really did Van Buren in ("Eight" nightmare, but common pattern, to have lost money). Not being re-elect-ed was a crushing blow, particularly for a Sag that thrives on the attention that comes from rooms full of parties (or politicians).

George Washington—1789-97

birthdate: 2/22/1732—Pisces, 1, Only (fifth but ten year difference)
Martha Dandridge Custis Washington
birthdate: 6/2/1731—Gemini, 11/2, Oldest girl

WASHINGTONS — NEW BEGINNINGS:

Martha was educated in reading and writing but was only encouraged to run a household effectively. When her husband was called to arms, she joined him to help the sick, and make the soldiers more comfortable. Then Washington was elected as President and it was Martha's job to set precedents on how to be a First Lady. Her witty Gemini personality and "Eleven/Two" negotiating skills would come in handy. George, being a "One" and goal-oriented Only child, would be responsible for establishing this new position. Washington created a cabinet, raised funds through taxes to break ties with England and more. Being number "One" in this higher ranking office worked the first time around but seemed less likely to be effective in following years.

Woodrow Wilson—1913-21

> birthdate: 12/28/1856—Capricorn, 6, Middle (third of four)
> Ellen Louise Axson Wilson
> birthdate: 5/15/1860—Taurus, 8, Unknown
> Edith Bolling Galt Wilson
> birthdate: 10/15/1872—Libra, 7, Middle (7th of eleven)

WILSON — DRIVEN AND DEDICATED:

Woodrow was a well-educated "Six" and created many tools to serve society (including being the president of Princeton and writing ten plus books). He held office when the 18th (Prohibition) and 19th (women's suffrage) constitutional amendments were adopted, instituted the Selective Service to draft able-bodied men (3 million), aggressively promoted the League of Nations which eventually evolved into United Nations. A driven Capricorn, he couldn't complete his League of Nations tour due to a stroke (another "Six" health issue) that nearly took his life and paralyzed him on one side. Wilson was known for relying on women for counsel (three daughters and two trusted, confident wives). Ellen was an artist and went to New York on her own to study (very independent "Eight" move during these times). Before she completed her studies, she married Woodrow and put her passion on hold to raise her family (Taurus focused) but encouraged him to run for offices and advised him on speeches and entertained influential politicians ("Eight" it up). Once her children grew, she spent more time painting and exhibiting her work. It became her mission to get decent housing for the poor and she sponsored a bill to improve these conditions. On her deathbed (dying of kidney disease), she said she could "go away more peacefully" if her bill was passed. The lawmakers passed this immediately and it became the "Ellen Wilson's bill." Woodrow was lost and lonely without his feminine balance but met another independent woman in 1915, Edith (Pocahontas was her ancestor), Libra balancer and "Seven" intellectual, well-to-do widow who managed a successful jewelry business and the first woman in Washington D.C. to get her driver's license. He installed a phone from the White House to her home so that he could discuss his presidential problems. Once he had the stroke, Edith guarded him from stress, would decide who he would and would not see and many guessed that she was really running the show for the balance of his term (calling it the "petticoat government").

VI.
So What Have We Learned?

"Where there is much desire to learn, there of necessity will be much arguing, much writing, many opinions; for opinions in good (wo)men is but knowledge in the making."

—Milton, Areopagitica (1644)

What I have learned is that we all have the same basic needs. We simply express them differently. We really aren't that complex. The key is balance of the "ALLNESS"—the masculine and feminine, ying and yang, or opposites. There are two sides to every coin. When you get a clearer understanding of your and others' core motivations then there is less struggle and increased balance. It seems the world lacks tolerance and that translates to judgment that others are incorrect (not matching judgers' "truths"). One way to heal this wound is to develop patience, understanding, respect, acknowledgement and appreciation for others' differences.

So let's be honest with ourselves, not one of us is the gold standard! Be clear that when you judge, it's coming right back at ya. So why generate that type of energy? Instead of repeating negative patterns, take a snapshot of yourself and those you come in contact with. Use this book and begin with who you are in connection with your Birth Mix. What acceleration points do you have? What season will be your best this year? Lay your profile next to others. Why don't you get along? Or maybe you get along fine and want to understand your significant other, siblings, children, parents, neighbors, friends… to strengthen your bond. Ask, "How do I bring out the best in myself and others? How can I enhance relationships?" Create a starting point of understanding utilizing these simple Birth Mix tools—Astrology, Numerology, Birth Order, and Earth Cycles.

Remember that this isn't about embracing any type of religion. It's simply another idea to manifest your reality so that your life flows effortlessly.

Love yourself. Appreciate others as best you can. It's not a perfect world so if you can't appreciate certain others, at least understand why you are not in the cosmic space to do so. You will find your patience and appreciation will increase over time.

I've provided some answers. Not all. These ideas may help your life flow a bit easier. If there are just a few pearls that reach you—give you that "ah ha" moment—then I am truly blessed.

Thanks for supporting my work. Now it's time to do yours!

About the Author

Photo by Pat Barcas

Michelle began to better understand the importance of targeting interests and needs of individuals through writing and creative pursuits in corporate America beginning in 1985. Mind, body, soul health became a more pressing need when she decided to strike out on her own in 1996 as a Wholistic Professional and Writer. She was led to Asheville, NC in 2009 where her roots date back to the 1700's. This is where she established a successful wholistic and integrative practice and collaborations that focus on clients, students and communities finding their voices. In addition, Michelle is a college instructor specializing in English studies and College Transfer Success.

Michelle has an eclectic background with **mind over matter solutions specialties** that include: Doctor of Clinical Hypnosis / Hypnotherapy, Self-Hypnosis, EFT (Emotional Freedom Technique), NLP (Neuro-Linguistic Programming), Acupressure Hypnosis, Past Life Regression, and Writing Coaching. Her **academic work** includes: teaching college English and College Transfer Success, a Master of Arts in English specializing in Rhetoric, Composition and Professional and Technical Writing, a Bachelor of Arts degree in Communication Arts, and various writing projects in academia. Other studies include how personality patterns are influenced by Astrology, Numerology, and Birth Order.

More information on Michelle's background, books, events, community collaborations, teaching, and her private practice can be found at www. MichellePayton.com, www.MichellePaytonWriter.com, www.TheLeftSide. com, or do an internet search on "Michelle Payton." She, her husband and life partner since 1982, and two of three grown children live, work and play in Asheville, North Carolina.

CONSCIOUS LIVING AND SELF-HELP BOOKS BY
M. A. (MICHELLE) PAYTON

As a mind over matter solutions professional and academic, Michelle's work focuses on how to accomplish 21st century, mindful living as a mainstream, as conscious as possible, work-in-progress parent, partner, professional, and individual, and how this has unfolded for her, her clients and throughout history.

Adventures of a Mainstream Metaphysical Mom: Choosing Peace of Mind in a World of Diverse Ideas (Book 1)

Mainstream metaphysical parenting, mentoring, and relationships with self and others in the 21st century!

2003 Finalist for Best Biographical/ Self-Help Book

—Coalition of Visionary Resources, 2003 Visionary Awards, International New Age Trade Show

192 pp ~ paperback
ISBN 978-0-9719804-0-2
$13.95

"Soul"utions: Achieving Financial, Intellectual, Physical, Social, and Spiritual Balance with Soul

Tips on soul-based living using goal setting principles in all areas of life!

239 pp ~ paperback
ISBN 978-0-9719804-1-9
$14.95

Birth Mix Patterns™: *Astrology, Numerology, and Birth Order, and their Effects on the Past, Present, and Future*

Analyzes hundreds of historical figures, including United States Presidents and First Ladies, artists, authors, civil rights leaders, and more in connection with astrology, numerology, and birth order.

2006 Finalist for Best General Interest/How To Book

—Coalition of Visionary Resources, 2006 Visionary Awards, International New Age Trade Show

160 pp ~ paperback

ISBN: 978-0-9719804-2-6

$12.95

Birth Mix Patterns™: *Astrology, Numerology, and Birth Order, and their Effects on the Families & Other Groups that Matter*

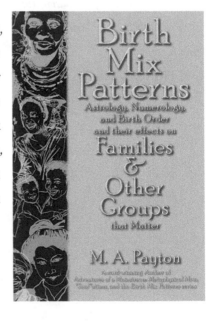

Analyzes the authors of the Declaration of Independence, dark leaders, the US Supreme Court Justices, the Beatles and more in connection with astrology, numerology, and birth order.

133 pp ~ paperback

ISBN 978-0-9719804-3-3

$12.95

Birth Mix Patterns™ and Loving Relationships using Astrology, Numerology, and Birth Order

Analyzes more than two dozen famous couples from Hollywood, to community servers, to same gender partnerships in connection with astrology, numerology, and birth order.

137 pp ~ paperback
ISBN 978-0-9719804-4-0
$12.95

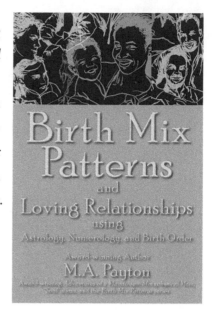

Healing What's Real: Expanding Your Personal Power with Mind Over Matter Techniques

Dr. Payton shares her experiences with Hypnotherapy, Neuro-Linguistic Programming™ (NLP), Emotional Freedom Technique™ (EFT), meditation, and more with dozens of transcribed sessions and interviews combining these techniques.

253 pp ~ paperback
ISBN 978-0-9719804-5-7
$15.95

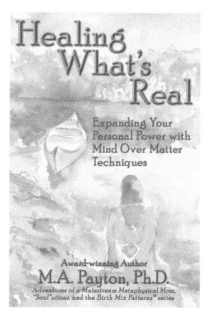

More Adventures of a Mainstream Metaphysical Mom: Finding Peace While Raising Teens, Building a Community, and Consciously Following-Through (Book 2)

More on mainstream metaphysical parenting, mentoring, and relationships as she and her family age and wade through constant changes and few hard and fast rules.

225 pp ~ paperback
ISBN-13: 978-0-9719804-6-4
$12.95

Writing Sensorably: How Expressive and Natural Voice Advance Recording Thoughts

Those interested in ways to record as much content as possible prior to the polish stage of a final document can begin with the natural speaking voice. Processes shared marry natural expression with practical steps that enhance: self-help processing, scientific observations, creative writing, journaling, descriptive work using multiple senses, and technical or methodical work with an interest in how published papers and research support out-of-the-box processes.

131 pp ~ paperback, ISBN-13: 978-0-9719804-7-1, $13.95
131 pp ~ Kindle Edition (e-book), ISBN-13: 978-09719804-8-8, $6.99

Positive Hypnosis: Re-associating with Solution-based Memories

All experiences create unique realities for each person, so when new information is absorbed into the human brain—like a perception that something doesn't work, re-connections to past experiences must be strong enough to re-position beliefs and habits. Those who are interested in self-empowerment using mind over matter techniques will find facts in

Positive Hypnosis on how the brain learns through re-association and why blocks occur in a healthy brain, why re-association is a key to individual re-thinking, and how Hypnosis, Self-Hypnosis and Neuro-linguistic Programming are experienced every day to dispel the perception of being controlled.

64 pp ~ paperback, ISBN 978-0-9719804-9-5, $12.95
64 pp ~ Kindle Edition (e-book), ISBN 978-0-9992426-0-5, $4.99

Quotations:

Index and Resources

Arc, Joan of
http://www.aolsvc.worldbook.aol.com/wb/Article?id=ar288800
http://www.facade.com/celebrity/Joan_of_Arc/
http://members.aol.com/hywwebsite/private/joanofarc.html
Born: January 6, 1412 — Life Path 6, Capricorn, Birth Order unknown/had siblings

Allen, Woody
http://www.imdb.com/name/nm0000095/
Born: December 1, 1935—Life Path 4, Sagittarius, Birth Order
unknown

Ali, Muhammad
http://www.facade.com/celebrity/Muhammad_Ali/
Born: January 17, 1942 — Life Path 7, Capricorn, Birth Order unknown

Andrews, Julie
http://www.imdb.com/name/nm0000267/
http://www.julieandrews.co.uk/biog.htm
Born: October 1, 1935 — Life Path 11/2, Libra, Birth Order unknown

Balch, Emily
http://nobelprize.org/peace/laureates/1946/balch-bio.html
Born: January 8, 1867 — Life Path 4, Capricorn, Birth Order unknown

Bell, Alexander Graham
http://www.lucidcafe.com/library/96mar/bell.html
Born: March 3, 1847—Life Path 8, Pisces, Birth Order unknown

Birthdate references (other than already referenced)
Kepler Software, version 4.6

Birth Order references
http://ourworld.compuserve.com/homepages/hstein/birthord.htm
http://www.childdevelopmentinfo.com/development/birth_order.htm
http://www.birthorderplus.com/birthorder/five.htm

"The New Birth Order," Dr. Kevin Leman, Presidents' Birth Orders, Pages 349-351, Ninth printing, November 2002

Bonaparte, Napoleon Emperor
http://www.geocities.com/CollegePark/Den/7664/naplifehistory.html
Born: August 15, 1769 — Life Path 1, Leo, Second son

Calderone, Mary
http://www.wic.org/bio/calderon.htm
Born: July 1, 1904 — Life Path 4, Cancer, Birth Order unknown

Carraway, Hattie Wyatt
http://bioguide.congress.gov/scripts/biodisplay.pl?index=C000138
Born: February 1, 1878 — Life Path 9, Aquarius, Birth Order unknown

Cassatt, Mary
http://www.biography.com/impressionists/artists_cassatt.html
Born: May 22, 1844 — Life Path 8, Gemini (Taurus cusp), Birth Order unknown

Chatman Catt, Carrie
Biography courtesy of the U.S. Library of Congress and the National 19th Amendment Society. www.catt.org/ccabout.html
Born: January 9, 1859 — Life Path 6, Capricorn, Middle Child

Connery, Sean Sir
http://www.imdb.com/name/nm0000125/
http://www.seanconnery.com/biography/
Born: August 25, 1930 — Life Path 1, Virgo, Oldest of two boys

Curie, Marie Dr.
http://nobelprize.org/physics/laureates/1903/marie-curie-bio.html
Born: November 7, 1867 — Life Path 4, Scorpio, Birth Order unknown

Da Vinci, Leonardo
http://www.kausal.com/leonardo/
Born: April 15, 1452 — Life Path 3, Aries, Only child

Darwin, Charles
http://oz.plymouth.edu/~biology/history/darwin.html
Born: February 12, 1809—Life Path 5, Aquarius, Birth Order unknown

Day O'Connor, Sandra http://www.aolsvc.worldbook.aol.com/wb/Arti-

cle?id=ar399040&sc=-1
http://www.lucidcafe.com/library/96mar/oconnor.html
Born: March 26, 1930 — Life Path 6, Aries, Birth Order unknown

Dickinson, Emily
http://www.cswnet.com/~erin/edbio.htm
http://www.online-literature.com/dickinson/
Born: December 10, 1830 — Life Path 7, Sagittarius, Birth Order unknown

Darwin, Charles
http://www2.lucidcafe.com/lucidcafe/library/96feb/darwin.html
Born: February 12, 1809 — Life Path 5, Aquarius, Middle child (second son of five)

Disney, Walt
http://www.justdisney.com/walt_disney/biography/w_bio_short.html
Born: December 5, 1901 — Life Path 1, Sagittarius, Birth Order unknown

Dole, Elizabeth
http://dole.senate.gov/index.cfm?FuseAction=AboutElizabeth.Biography
http://www.who2.com/elizabethdole.html
http://www.msnbc.com/onair/nbc/today/birthorder/political.asp?cp1=1 (indicating youngest of two children with another website referring to her brother)
Born: July 29, 1936 — Life Path 1, Leo, Only (approximately 15 year older brother)

Earhart, Amelia
Bilstein, Roger E. "Earhart, Amelia." World Book Online Reference Center. 2004. World Book, Inc. 23 Apr. 2004. http://www.aolsvc.worldbook.aol.com/wb/Article?id=ar171340>.
http://ellensplace.net/ae_eyrs.html
Born: July 24, 1897 — Life Path 2, Leo (Cancer cusp), Oldest of two (girls)

Edison, Thomas
http://www.thomasedison.com/biog.htm
http://www.vcsc.k12.in.us/th/hagen/invent/Edison.htm
Born: February 11, 1847 — Life Path 6, Aquarius, Youngest of six siblings

Einstein, Albert
http://en.wikipedia.org/wiki/Albert_Einstein
Born: March 14, 1879—Life Path 6, Pisces, Oldest

Ford, Betty
http://www.ford.utexas.edu/grf/bbfbiop.htm
Born: 4/8/1918 — Aries, 4, Oldest/Only daughter (third child)

Flanner, Janet
http://www.bsu.edu/ourlandourlit/Literature/Authors/flannerj.htm
http://www.loc.gov/exhibits/wcf/wcf0011.html
Born: March 13, 1892 — Life Path 9, Pisces, Birth Order unknown

Foster, Jodie
http://www.imdb.com/name/nm0000149/
Born: November 19, 1962—Life Path 3, Scorpio, Birth Order unknown

Frank, Anne
http://www.annefrank.com/1_life.htm
http://www.geocities.com/afdiary/people.htm
http://www.thehistorychannel.co.uk/site/features/anne_frank.php
Born: June 12, 1929 — Life Path 3, Gemini, Youngest (with older sister)

Gandhi, Mohandas
http://web.mahatma.org.in/familytree/familytree.jsp?link=ft
Born: 10/2/1869 — Life Path 9, Libra, Youngest (of father's fourth wife)

Gates, Bill
http://en.wikipedia.org/wiki/Bill_Gates
Born: October 28, 1955—Life Path 4, Scorpio, Birth Order unknown

Glenn, John
http://www.enchantedlearning.com/explorers/page/g/glenn.shtml
Born: July 18, 1921—Life Path 2, Cancer, Birth Order unknown

Horne, Lena
http://music.channel.aol.com/artist/artistbio.adp?_pgtyp=&artistid=6769
http://www.geocities.com/BourbonStreet/Delta/6424/biography.html
Born: June 30, 1917 — Life Path 9, Leo, Only child

Hughes, Howard
http://www.rotten.com/library/bio/business/howard-hughes/
http://www.allsands.com/Entertainment/People/howardhughesbi_amm_gn.htm
Born: September 24, 1905 (Note: other research shows claims of inaccurate reports of Howard Hughes birth December 24, 1905) — Life Path 3, Libra (Virgo cusp), Only child

Hurkos, Peter
http://www.astrotheme.fr/en/celebrites/lune_ascendant_10_2.htm
Born: May 21, 1911—Life Path 11/2, Taurus (cusp Gemini), Birth Order unknown

Kennedy Jr., John
http://www.infoplease.com/spot/kennedybio.html
Born: November 25, 1960—Life Path 7, Sagittarius, Oldest boy (one sister)

King, Stephen
http://en.wikipedia.org/wiki/Stephen_King#Biography
Born: September 21, 1947—Life Path 6, Virgo, Youngest (of two boys)

King, Coretta Scott
www.who2.com/corettascottking.html
http://www.stanford.edu/group/King/about_king/details/270427b.htm
http://www2.lhric.org/pocantico/womenenc/king3.htm
Born: April 27, 1927 — Life Path 5, Taurus, Three girls (order unknown)

King Jr., Martin Luther
http://en.wikipedia.org/wiki/Martin_Luther_King,_Jr.
http://www.mccsc.edu/~kmcglaun/mlk/bio.htm
Born: January 15, 1929—Life Path 1, Capricorn, Middle (second son, of three boys, two years older and younger to him)

Lama, Dalai (14th)
http://www.tibet.com/DL/biography.html
Born: July 6, 1935 — Life Path 22, Cancer, Raised as Only (taken by age of two from peasant home)

Lee, Bruce
http://www.geocities.com/Colosseum/Track/5996/bio.html
http://www.personal.psu.edu/users/a/m/amf234/Bruce%20Lee.html
Born: November 27, 1940—Life Path 7, Sagittarius, Seven siblings

Lennon, John
http://webhome.idirect.com/~faab/AbbeyRoad/john4.htm
Born: October 9, 1940—Life Path 6, Libra, Birth Order unknown

Lewis, Jerry
http://www.eonline.com/On/Holly/Shows/Lewis/bio.html
Born: March 16, 1926—Life Path 1, Pisces, Birth Order unknown

Lindbergh, Charles
http://www.acepilots.com/lindbergh.html
Born: February 4, 1902—Life Path 9, Aquarius, Only (two half sisters much older than him)

Mansfield-Sullivan, Anne
Stuckey, Kenneth A. "Sullivan, Anne Mansfield." World Book Online Reference Center. 2004. World Book, Inc. 23 Apr. 2004. <http://www.aolsvc.worldbook.aol.com/wb/Article?id=ar538800>.
Born: April 14, 1866 — Life Path 3, Aries, Oldest (two younger siblings/boy and girl)

Michelangelo
http://www.rsm.ac.uk/new/pdfs/j05-04michelangelo.pdf
Born: March 6, 1475—Life Path 8, Pisces, Middle (second oldest of five boys)

Mitchell, Maria
http://www.lkwdpl.org/wihohio/mitc-mar.htm
Born: August 1, 1818 — Life Path 9, Leo, Middle (third child of ten)

Monroe, Marilyn
http://www.everlasting-star.net/biography.php
Born: June 1, 1926—Life Path 7, Gemini, Only patterns probable (grew up in various foster homes, dysfunctional shuffling as a child)

Montessori, Maria
1. Kramer, R. "Maria Montessori," Fifth Printing, November 1996, 23-36.
Born: August 31, 1870 — Life Path 1, Virgo, Only Child

Mozart, Wolfgang
http://www.britannica.com/eb/article?tocId=9108745
http://apacheel.peoriaud.k12.az.us/Arts%20Discovery%202002/Mozart-Laura%20Shulz.pps
Born: January 27, 1756—Life Path 11, Aquarius, Oldest boy (six siblings but only two survived—him and a sister)

Murphy, Eddie
http://www.imdb.com/name/nm0000552/bio
Born: April 3, 1961—Life Path 6, Aries, Youngest son first marriage (of two boys from mother's first marriage, had a step-brother versus blood brother from mother's second marriage)

Newton, Sir Isaac
http://www-groups.dcs.st-and.ac.uk/~history/Mathematicians/Newton.html
Born: January 4, 1643 — Life Path 1, Capricorn, Oldest

Nightengale, Florence
Florence Nightengale Museum, London, http://www.florence-nightingale.co.uk/flo2.htm, 2004
Born: May 12, 1820 — Life Path 1, Taurus, Younger of two girls (one year apart)

Numerology, Resource material includes references to Hans Decoz Numerology (www.decoz.com)

Parks, Rosa
http://teacher.scholastic.com/researchtools/articlearchives/honormlk/rosa.htm
http://www.thebiographychannel.co.uk/new_site/biography.php?id=446&show-group=740
http://www.girlpower.gov/girlarea/gpguests/RosaParks.htm
http://www.east-buc.k12.ia.us/00_01/BH/rp/rp.htm
http://rosaparks.netfirms.com/
Born: February 4, 1913 — Life Path 11, Aquarius, Oldest girl (had younger brother)

Paul, Alice
http://womenshistory.about.com/library/bio/blbio_paul_alice.htm
Born: January 11, 1885—Life Path 7, Capricorn, Birth Order unknown

Paul, Pope John II
http://www.zpub.com/un/pope/unpope-bio.html
Born: May 18, 1920—Life Path 8, Taurus, Birth Order unknown

Presley, Elvis
http://www.facade.com/celebrity/Elvis_Presley/
http://www.history-of-rock.com/elvis_presley.htm
Born: January 8, 1935 — Life Path 9, Capricorn, Only (twin died at birth)

Rankin, Jeanette
http://www.salsa.net/peace/faces/rankin.html
http://www.spartacus.schoolnet.co.uk/USArankin.htm
Born: June 11, 1880 — Life Path 7, Gemini, Birth Order unknown

Ride, Dr. Sally http://starchild.gsfc.nasa.gov/docs/StarChild/whos_who_level2/ride.html
Born: May 26, 1951 — Life Path 2, Gemini, Birth Order unknown

Rockerfeller, John D. Sr.
http://www2.lhric.org/pocantico/rockefeller/events.htm
http://www.geocities.com/beckyok2/JohnDRockefeller.html
Born: July 8, 1839—Life Path 9, Cancer, Five brothers and sisters

Rockwell, Norman
http://www.illustration-house.com/bios/rockwell_bio.html
http://www.lucidcafe.com/library/96feb/rockwell.html
Born: February 3, 1894 — Life Path 9, Aquarius, Birth Order unknown

Ruth, Babe
http://www.baberuth.com/flash/about/biograph.html
Born: February 6, 1895—Life Path 4, Aquarius, Oldest boy (eight children but only two survived past infancy, one boy and one girl, but by seven years of age sent to reformatory and rarely visited)

Schwarzenegger, Arnold
http://german.about.com/library/blaschwarz.htm
Born: July 30, 1947—Life Path 4, Leo, Second son

Shakespeare, William
http://www.allshakespeare.com/bio/47408
Born: between April 23 and 26 (his baptism day), 1564 — Life Path Not Available, Taurus, Oldest

Spencer, Lady Diana, Princess of Wales http.//www.who2.com/charlesprinceofwales. html http://www.royal.gov.uk/output/page155.asp, http://www.royal.gov.uk/output/ page153.asp, 2004
Born: July 1, 1961 — Life Path 7, Cancer, Middle (two older sisters and younger brother)

Spielberg, Steven
http://www.imdb.com/name/nm0000229/bio
Born: December 18, 1946—Life Path 5, Sagittarius, Oldest (of four, three girls)

Steinem, Gloria
http://www.nwhp.org/tlp/biographies/steinem/steinem_bio.html
Born: March 25, 1934—Life Path 9, Aries, Only (sister ten years older than her)

Taylor, Elizabeth http://www.geocities.com/Hollywood/Guild/7634/taylor.html, Biography by Denny Jackson, 2004
Born: February 27, 1932 — Life Path 8, Pisces, Birth Order unknown

Tchaikovsky, Peter
http://www.balletmet.org/Notes/Tchaikovsky.html
Born: May 7, 1840—Life Path 7, Taurus, Second oldest of six

Tubman, Harriet
http://www.nyhistory.com/harriettubman/life.htm
Born: March 26, 1819 or 1820 — Life Path Not Available, Aries, Birth Order unknown

Trump, Donald
http://people.aol.com/people/searchresults/1,20109,,00.html?search=donald+trump
http://en.wikipedia.org/wiki/Donald_Trump#Family
Born: June 14, 1946 — Life Path 4, Gemini, Middle (fourth of five children)

Twain, Mark (Samuel Clemens)
http://www.online-literature.com/twain/
http://www.marktwainmuseum.org/JMC.html
Born November 30, 1835 — Life Path 22, Sagittarius, Youngest of six

U.S. Presidents References:
"Fandex, Family Field Guides, Presidents" by Workman Publishing New York, copyright 1997
http://www.whitehouse.gov/history/presidents
http://www.americanpresidents.org/
http://www.americanpresident.org/
"The New Birth Order" by Dr. Kevin Leman, Presidents' Birth Orders, pages 349-351, ninth printing; November 2002

U.S. First Ladies References:
"Fandex, Family Field Guides, First Ladies" by Workman Publishing New York, copyright 1997
http://www.whitehouse.gov/history/firstladies

Van Gogh, Vincent
http://www.vangoghgallery.com/misc/bio.htm
http://webexhibits.org/vangogh/memoir/sisterinlaw/2.html
Born: March 30, 1853—Life Path 5, Aries, Oldest but said to be sickly (of four boys and three girls)

Wayne, John
http://www.imdb.com/name/nm0000078/
Born: May 26, 1907—Life Path 3, Gemini, Oldest (of two boys)

Willard, Frances
http://search.eb.com/women/articles/Willard_Frances_Elizabeth_Caroline.html
Born: September 28, 1839 — Life Path 4, Libra, Birth Order unknown

Winfrey, Oprah
http://www.achievement.org/autodoc/page/winobio-1
http://www.oprah.com. Biographical section of "official Oprah Winfrey" website.
Born: January 29, 1954 — Life Path 4, Aquarius, Only (raised as Only due to constant moving around/lived with Mother and one half-sister for a short time)

Windsor, Charles, Prince of Wales (heir to the Throne of England)
http://www.who2.com/charlesprinceofwales.html
Born: November 14, 1948 — Life Path 11, Scorpio, Oldest

Wonder, Stevie
http://www.facade.com/celebrity — celebrity birthdates
http://askmen.com/men/entertainment_100/119c_stevie_wonder.html
Born: May 13, 1950 — Life Path 6, Taurus, Five siblings

CPSIA information can be obtained
at www.ICGtesting.com
Printed in the USA
BVHW041854170219
540481BV00015B/285/P

9 780971 980426